AUTISM &
EDUCATION

THE WAY   I SEE IT

DR. TEMPLE
GRANDIN

What Parents and Teachers Need to Know

AUTISM & EDUCATION: THE WAY I SEE IT

All marketing and publishing rights guaranteed to and reserved by:

FUTURE HORIZONS

(817) 277-0727

(817) 277-2270 (fax)

E-mail: info@fhautism.com

www.fhautism.com

ISBN: 9781957984070

CONTENTS

CHAPTER TWO

CONTENTS

FOREWORD

ANSWERS TO THE MOST COMMON RECENT QUESTIONS

BY TEMPLE GRANDIN

In this book focusing on education, it is important to address some recent concerns that have been raised by adults who are on the autism spectrum. I also want to help parents and teachers to avoid getting locked into the label of autism and failing to see the whole child. The abilities of autistic children are often underestimated.

Today, many parents who receive a diagnosis that their young child has autism may find many conflicting viewpoints on the best type of therapy. Autism specialists all agree that young two- to five-year-old children who are not talking should receive therapy. The worst thing a parent can do is to do nothing and allow the child to zone out on electronic devices. The child should immediately start therapy. If therapy is not available, a student or a grandparent could volunteer to work with the child.

Some autistic adults have websites and other online media where they adamantly oppose the use of ABA (Applied Behavior Analysis) as a treatment for autism. Studies show that modern ABA is an evidence-based treatment for very young children. Some of these advocates were subjected to harsh, punitive ABA that forced them into sensory overload. In these poor programs, there was also too much emphasis on compliance and not enough work on developing the child's abilities.

There is another recent development that may make some autistic treatment programs a poor choice. Since ABA is covered by insurance, private equity firms have recently purchased ABA practices. They discovered that these clinics were a lucrative financial investment. This may provide an economic incentive to teach all children with the same "cookie cutter" program. A good ABA clinic will carefully tailor each program to fit the needs of each child. The incentive for more insurance dollars may also motivate a clinic to recommend excessive amounts of therapy. They may also use poorly trained staff to handle big caseloads.

How to Evaluate Effective Early Educational Program for a Young Nonverbal Child

Little kids between the ages of two to five who are not talking need about ten to twenty hours a week of one-to-one teaching with an effective teacher. That teacher could be an ABA therapist, an occupational therapist, a speech therapist, a parent, or a grandparent. I have observed that effective teachers have a "knack" for engaging the child and making progress. There are four simple ways to evaluate the effectiveness of a teacher for a child under five years of age:

1. The child learns more and more speech.
2. The child learns how to wait and take turns at games. This is an important skill to learn because it helps the child to reduce impulsive behavior.
3. The child learns more and more skills such as hand washing, eating with utensils, and putting on a jacket.
4. The child should like going to therapy. If the child hates therapy, the program must be changed.

FOREWORD

Recommendations for Older Children and Answers to Recent Common Questions

By the time I was five, I had learned to talk and I no longer needed one-to-one therapy with a teacher. I am concerned that a clinic that is making money from insurance may have an economic incentive to continue intensive therapy when it should be phased out. If a child does not quickly learn language, they must be provided with an alternative method to communicate, such as sign language, an electronic augmentative communication device, or a picture board. I can remember the total frustration of not being able to communicate. Sometimes I attempted to communicate by screaming. Meltdowns and aggression may be triggered by either a lack of a method to communicate or sensory overload. Some autistic individuals are more likely to become aggressive in noisy environments. Their sensory system may be more sensitive to sudden loud noise.

Another common question I get asked is "Should a child be allowed to stim?" Stimming is repetitive behavior such as rocking or spinning objects. I was allowed to stim for an hour after lunch and again in the evening. It helped to calm me down. I was not allowed to stim at the dining room table. Another common recent question is about "masking" (camouflaging) and suppressing autistic behavior. Masking is used to appear more normal. For example, I learned not to bite my fingernails in front of other people. I have replaced stims, such as spinning an object, with intricate doodles I do on a piece of paper. This "stim" does not bother other people. When I was younger, I used my squeeze machine every day to calm down. It is described in detail in my book *Thinking in Pictures*. The use of deep pressure and other effective sensory methods is covered in several chapters in this book. Some people wanted to take my squeeze machine away. That would have been very detrimental to me. Another calming method was watching old *Star Trek* episodes in the late afternoon to help me chill.

Another common question is about autistic burnout in young adults. Many advocates maintain that this is caused by constantly having to "mask" autistic behavior to appear more normal. In many of my publications, I have written about serious problems with panic attacks and anxiety. During my twenties, they got worse. By the time I was in my early thirties, my health was deteriorating due to constant colitis. The stress caused by panic attacks was damaging my body. A complete description of my symptoms is in *Thinking in Pictures*. My symptoms may be similar to the autistic burnout that is described by some adult advocates. Starting a low dose of an antidepressant in my early thirties greatly reduced my anxiety. My colitis issues were almost eliminated. This may have helped me avoid autistic burnout. There are extensive discussions of medications in this edition of *The Way I See It* and in *Thinking in Pictures*. I have been on the same low dose of an antidepressant for forty years. It is likely that my health would have really deteriorated if I had not discovered the use of antidepressants.

I want to emphasize that way too many medications are given to young children. Parents have told me about elementary school age kids who were on four to seven medications. Discussions with them often indicated that every time the child had a behavior problem, another prescription was added. This is bad because some medications have severe side effects, such as obesity.

Recently, I attended a meeting where autistic adults discussed masking. Another cause of burnout may be social situations where there is rapid back-and-forth chitchat. I do not have sufficient brain processing speed to follow these conversations. I usually avoid the evening happy hours that contain them. Some people at the meeting also had problems with hearing in noisy environments. Others and I at this meeting agreed that learning some basic social skills, such as being polite, is not difficult and that some masking is necessary to survive. One woman said there is a fine line between doing some minor masking and suppressing her identity. I express my identity by wearing western clothes, but I had to learn to be clean and polite.

The happiest autistic adults I have known have careers they love, where they have lots of friends through shared interests. For me, the best conversations are about interesting subjects such as animal behavior, construction, autism, and brain research. *Autism and Education: The Way I See It* will help autistic children and adults to achieve their full potential.

Further Reading

Advisory.com (2022) Private equity in autism care: The advantages and trade-offs, www.advisory.com/dailybriefing/2022/08/16/autism-private-equity.

ASAN – Our motto: What is "nothing about us without us?" https://autisticadvocacy.org/about-asan/what-we-believe/.

Bannow, T. (2022) Parents and clinicians say private equity's profit fixation is short changing kids with autism, www.statnews.com/2022/08/15/private-equity-autism-aba-therapy/.

Bascom, J. (2020) Problematic and traumatic: Why nobody needs ABA, https://autisticselfadvocaatesagainstaba.wordpress.com/2020/04/13/problematic-andtraumatic-why-nobody-needs-aba/

Cook, J. et al. (2021) Camouflaging in autism: A systematic review, *Clinical Psychology Review*, Vol. 89, 102080.

Danesh, A.A. et al. (2021) Hyperacusis in Autism Spectrum Disorders, *Audiology Research*, 11:547-556.

Fry, E. (2022) Private equity is the biggest plyer in the booming autism therapy industry: Some therapists say the money grab is hurting the quality of care, Fortune.com.

Leaf, J.B. et al. (2022) Concerns about ABA based interventions: An evaluation and recommendation, *Journal of Autism and Developmental Disorders*, 52(6):2838-2853.

University of California, San Francisco. First-hand perspectives on behavioral intervention for autistic people and people with other developmental disorders, https://odpc.ucsf.edu/training/best-practices-behaviorsupport/first-hand-perspctives-on-behavioral-interventions-for-autisticpeople.

Van der Boogert, F. et al. (2021) Sensory processing and aggressive behavior in adults with autism spectrum disorder, *Brain Science*, 11(1)95.

Yu, Q. et al. (2020) Efficacy of interventions based on applied behavior analysis for autism spectrum disorder: A meta-analysis, *Psychiatry Investigation*, 17(5):432-443.

CHAPTER  ONE

THE IMPORTANCE OF EARLY EDUCATIONAL INTERVENTION

The best thing a parent of a newly diagnosed child can do is to watch their child, without preconceived notions and judgments, and learn how the child functions, acts, and reacts to his or her world.

Both research and practical experience show that an intensive early education program in which a young child receives a minimum of twenty hours a week of instruction from a skilled teacher greatly improves prognosis. The brain of the young child is still growing and evolving. At this age, the neural pathways are highly malleable, and intensive instruction can reprogram "faulty wiring" that prevents the child from learning. Plus, behaviors in a young child have not yet become ingrained. It will take less practice to change an inappropriate behavior at age two to three than it will to change the same behavior at age seven to eight. By then, the child has had many years of doing things his way and change comes about more slowly.

For early childhood programs, ABA (applied behavioral analysis) programs using discrete trial training have the best scientific documentation backing up their use. But other programs, such as the Early Start Denver Model (ESDM), have been validated in a randomized trial. Additional evidence-based programs are pivotal response, speech therapy, and occupational therapy. The autism spectrum is vast and diversified. Children have different ways of thinking and processing information, and it is important that an intervention method be aligned with the child's learning profile and personality. Detailed descriptions of different types of early intervention programs can be found online.

A book I recommend is *Early Intervention and Autism: Real Life Questions, Real Life Answers* by Dr. James Ball (2012) from Future Horizons, Inc. While this book is written for parents of newly diagnosed children, more than 75 percent of the information on interventions, effective teaching strategies, program planning, and behavior management is valuable for parents of children of all ages.

My Early Intervention Program

I had a wonderful and effective early education program that started at age two and a half. By then, I had all the classic symptoms of autism, including no speech, no eye contact, tantrums, and constant repetitive behavior. This was in 1949, and doctors knew nothing about autism, but my mother would not accept that nothing could be done to help me. She was determined and knew that letting me continue without treatment would be the worst thing she could do. She obtained advice from a wise neurologist who referred her to a speech therapist to work with me. She was just as good as the autism specialists today.

My talented speech therapist worked with me for three hours a week doing ABA-type training (breaking skills down into small components, teaching each component separately using repetitive drills that gave me lots of practice) and she carefully enunciated hard consonant sounds so I could hear them. At the speech therapy school, I also attended a highly structured nursery school class with five or six other children who were not autistic. Several of the children had Down syndrome. These classes lasted about eight hours a week.

My nanny was another critical part of my early therapy. She spent 20 hours a week keeping me engaged. For instance, playing repeated turn-taking games with my sister and me. She was instrumental in introducing early social skills lessons, even though at that time, they weren't referred to as such in a formal manner. Within the realm of play, she kept me engaged and set up activities so that most involved turn-taking and lessons about being with others. In the winter, we went outdoors to play in the snow. She brought one sled and my sister and I had to take turns sledding down the hill. In the summer, we took turns on the swing. We were also taught to sit at the table and have good table manners. Teaching and learning opportunities were woven into everyday life.

When I turned five, we played lots of board games such as Parcheesi and Chinese checkers. My interest in art and making things was actively encouraged and I did many art projects. For most of the day, I was forced to keep my brain tuned into the world. However, my mother realized that my behaviors served a purpose and that changing those behaviors didn't happen overnight. I was given one hour after lunch where I could revert back to repetitive autistic behaviors without consequence. During this hour, I had to stay in my room. I sometimes spent the entire time spinning a decorative brass plate that covered a bolt that held my bed frame together. I would spin it at different speeds and was fascinated at how different speeds affected the number of times the brass plate spun.

The best thing a parent of a newly diagnosed child can do is to watch their child without preconceived notions and judgments and learn how the child functions, acts, and reacts to his or her world. My book, *Navigating Autism*, will help prevent parents from becoming label-locked and underestimating the abilities of their child. That information is invaluable in finding an intervention method that will be a good match to the child's learning style and needs. The worst thing parents can do with a child between the ages of two to five is nothing. It doesn't matter if the child is formally diagnosed with autism spectrum disorder (ASD) or has been labeled something less defined, such as global developmental delay. It doesn't matter if the child is not yet diagnosed if there are signs that the child may be on the spectrum: speech is severely delayed, the child's behaviors are odd and repetitive, the child doesn't engage with people or his/her environment, etc. The child must not be allowed to sit around stimming all day or, conversely, tuning out the world around him/ her. Parents, hear this: doing nothing is the worst thing you can do. If you have a three-year-old with no speech who is showing signs of autistic behavior, you need to start working with your child now. If signs are appearing in a child younger than three, even better. Do not wait six more months or a year even if your pediatrician is suggesting you take the "wait and see" approach or is plying you with advice such as "boys develop later than girls" or "not all children start to speak at the same time." My advice to act now is doubly emphasized if your child's language started developing late or his/ her language and/or behavior is regressing.

Parents can find themselves on long waiting lists for both diagnosis and early intervention services. In some cases, the child will age out of the state's early intervention system (birth to three) before his name gets to the top of the list! There is much parents can do to begin working with the child before formal professional intervention begins. Play turn-taking games and encourage eye contact. Grandparents who have lots of experience with children can be very effective. If you are unable to obtain professional services for your young child, you need to start working with your child immediately.

This book and Raun Kaufman's book, *Autism Breakthrough*, will be useful guides on how to work with young kids. The best part of Kaufman's book are the teaching guidelines that grandparents and other untrained people can easily use. Ignore his opinions about other treatments. Do not allow young children under five to zone out with tablets, phones, or other electronic devices. In young children, solitary screen time must be limited to one hour a day. For children under five, all other activities with electronic devices should be interactive activities done with a parent or teacher.

The intense interest in the electronic device can be used to motivate interest in doing a game where turns are taken with another person. During this game, the phone should be physically passed back and forth during turn taking. Too many kids are tuning out the world with electronics. In older children, video game playing should be limited to one hour a day. Excessive video gaming and screen use is a major problem in individuals with autism.

Engagement with the child at this point in time is just as effective as is instruction. While you may not yet be knowledgeable about various autism intervention models, you are smart enough and motivated enough to engage your child for 20 plus hours a week. Don't wait! Act now!

References and Additional Reading

Adele, D. (2017) The impact of delay of early intensive behavioral intervention on educational outcomes for a cohort of medicaid-enrolled children with autism, Dissertation, University of Minnesota.

Ball, J. (2012) *Early Intervention and Autism: Real Life Questions, Real Life Answers*, Future Horizons, Inc., Arlington, TX.

Children's Hospital of Philadelphia (2017) Evidence-based treatment options for Autism, www.chop.edu/news/evidence-based-treatment-options-autism (Accessed June 22, 2019).

Dawson, G. et al. (2010) Randomized controlled trial of an intervention for toddlers with autism: The Early Start Mode, *Pediatrics* 125:e17-e23.

Fuller E.A. et al. (2020) The effect of the early start Denver model for Children with Autism Spectrum Disorder: a Meta-analysis, *Brain Science*, 10(6) 368.

Grandin, T. (1996) *Emergence: Labeled Autistic*, Warner, Books, New York, NY.

Grandin, T. and Moore, D. (2021) *Navigating Autism: Nine Mindsets for Helping Kids on the Spectrum*, Norton Books, New York, NY.

Gengoux, G.W. et al. (2019) A pivotal response treatment package for children with autism spectrum disorder, *Pediatrics*, Sept:144(3) doi:10.1542/peds.2019-0178

Kaufman, R.K. (2015) *Autism Breakthrough*, St. Martin's Griffin.

Koegel, L. and Lazebnik, C. (2014) *Overcoming Autism: Finding Strategies and Hope That Can Transport a Child's Life*, Penguin Group, New York, NY.

Le, J. and Ventola, P. (2017) Pivotal response treatment for autism spectrum disorder: *Current Perspectives in Neuropsychiatric Disorders Treatment*, 13:1613-1626.

DO NOT GET TRAPPED BY LABELS

An autism diagnosis is not precise, like a diagnosis for a disease. I can get a lab test for cancer or tuberculosis that is very definitive; this is not true for autism. In the U.S., a diagnosis for autism is a behavioral profile based on a manual published by the American Psychiatric Association called the DSM (*Diagnostic and Statistical Manual of Mental Disorders*). The behavioral profiles in this manual are based on a combination of scientific studies and the opinion of a panel of expert doctors who debated in a conference room. A draft of the new ICD-11 (International Classification of Diseases) guidelines was published in 2019. It will be outlined in this chapter. Since the ICD is used in many countries around the world for all types of diseases, it is designed to be easily used by primary care doctors.

When Richard Panek and I worked on our book titled *The Autistic Brain* (2013), we reviewed the entire history of the DSM. Since the 1950s and 1960s, the diagnostic criteria for autism has changed dramatically. When all the changes made during the last 60 years are looked at side-by-side, it is rather shocking.

In 1980, a child had to have both speech delay and autistic behaviors to be diagnosed with autism. In 1994, Asperger's syndrome was added, in which the child is socially awkward with no speech delay. In the 2013 DSM-5, Asperger's syndrome (AS) and PDD-NOS (pervasive developmental disorder—not otherwise specified) were removed. These labels are now all merged into a broad autism spectrum disorder (ASD). There is no longer any requirement for speech delay. Taking out speech delay makes the DSM-5 more vague than the old DSM-IV. Some scientists do not consider language delay as a core symptom of autism because language delays and speech abnormalities are so variable.

For a person to be labeled with ASD, the DSM-5 requires that symptoms must be present in early childhood, but the age of onset is no longer defined. The DSM-5 whittles symptoms down to social and behavioral. The main emphasis is on social abnormalities inherent in the disorder: deficits in social interaction, reciprocal communication, and developing and keeping relationships with friends. In addition, the child must have two out of four of the following: repetitive behavior, adherence to routines, fixated interests, or sensory problems. Studies have shown that 91 percent of individuals with an Asperger's or PDD-NOS diagnosis will still qualify for an ASD diagnosis in the DSM-5. The DSM-5 also created a new social communication diagnosis, which consists of the social problems of ASD without the repetitive behavior, fixated interests, or sensory problems. To state that this is not autism does not make sense, because social deficits are a core autism symptom. Since there is no funding for social communication disorder, very few children have received this diagnosis.

Autism is a Huge Spectrum

One of the big problems with an autism diagnosis is that it has now changed to a broad spectrum with a wide-ranging degree of abilities.

The latest brain scan research by Aidas Aglinskas and colleagues (2022) at Boston College shows that the autism spectrum is a true continuous trait. As a child grows up, there is no black and white dividing line between slight nerdiness and mild autism. When children are really little (age two to five), most experts agree that many early educational treatments greatly improve prognosis. When I was three, I had no speech and all the typical autistic symptoms.

ABA-type (applied behavior analysis) speech therapy and turn-taking games made it possible for me to be enrolled in a regular kindergarten at age five.

Rebecca Grzadzinski, Marisela Huerta, and Catherine Lord (2013) stated, "In terms of cognitive functioning, individuals with ASD display a wide range of abilities from severe intellectual disability (ID) to superior intelligence."

Individuals with ASD range from computer scientists at Silicon Valley to individuals who will never live independently. They may not be able to participate in activities such as shopping trips or a sports event. When such a broad range of abilities is lumped together, it is difficult for special education teachers to shift gears between the different levels of abilities. Too often a child with superior abilities is placed in a classroom with more severely impaired students. This may hold this student back and not enable him/her to achieve.

Some people have switched to using the international ICD-10 diagnostic system, which still has the Asperger's label. An abbreviated definition of autism in the new ICD-11 is:

- Persistent deficits in initiating and sustaining social interactions.
- Restricted, repetitive, and inflexible patterns of behavior and interests.

When *The Way I See It* first went to press, a final draft of the ICD-11 had been published. The Asperger's label has been removed and autism is described with six levels of severity. I like the new ICD-11 draft because it provides clearer guidance. There is a heavy emphasis on whether or not the person has a disorder of intellectual development. When therapies are effective, a child or adult can progress to a higher level. Below is my simplified summary. You can access the complete ICD-11 online.

- Autism – Both without intellectual disability and normal language (formerly Asperger's diagnosis)
- Autism – Intellectual disability with normal or near-normal language.

- Autism – Without intellectual disability and with impaired functional language.
- Autism – Both impaired intellectual development and language.
- Autism – Without intellectual disability and no language.
- Autism – Intellectual disability and no language.

Bust Out of the Label Silos; ADHD and Autism Overlap

Each diagnostic label has its own support group meetings and books. Unfortunately, each group may stay in its own silo and there may be little communication between them. I have observed that the books for each diagnosis are almost all particular to that diagnosis. In many cases, there are kids who fit in more than one diagnosis. There are four diagnostic labels that get mixed up all the time. They are ASD, sensory processing disorder (SPD), ADHD (attention-deficit/hyperactivity disorder), and gifted. Both the DSM-5 and ICD-11 allow a dual diagnosis of ASD and ADHD.

In fact, three studies show that there is a genetic overlap with autism and ADHD. The biggest crossover in genetic factors is between fully verbal autism (Asperger's) and ADHD. This is why autism and ADHD are often mixed up. One doctor will give a child an autism diagnosis and another will diagnose that same child as ADHD. A neuro-imaging study shows that both autism and ADHD have similar structural abnormalities in the social parts of the brain. Some of these kids may be gifted in one academic subject and have a severe disability in another. Sometimes a child is labeled twice exceptional (or 2E) and he/she may be both gifted and have either an ASD, ADHD, or SPD diagnosis. When the same type of students get put in different silos, they often go down different paths.

My observations at conferences indicate that about half the children who are brought to an autism conference are gifted in at least one area such as math, music, reading, or art. In other chapters, I will discuss the need for developing their strengths. When I attend a gifted education conference, I see the same little geeky kids going down a different, very positive path toward a career in science or art. I want to make it very clear: geek, nerd, and mild ASD are the same thing. There is a point where being socially awkward is just part of normal human variation. There is fascinating new research that shows that autism may be the price for a human brain. The same genes that make the human brain large also cause autism. Other studies have shown that autistic traits are present in the general population.

I have also given talks at many high-tech companies, and it is likely that almost half the people who work there have mild ASD. One executive at a tech company told me that he knows they have many employees with ASD or mild ASD, but they don't talk about it. Many people in successful technical careers hate the ASD label because they feel that it implies that they are damaged. They avoid the labels. Recently I read about a young man who had a severe speech delay, and he was apprenticed into his father's physics lab. He had several scientific papers published before he was 20. If he had been born into a different situation, he may have taken a different path as an individual labeled with ASD.

Labels Required for School or Medical Services

Schools and insurance companies require diagnostic labels in order to get services. Unfortunately, I am seeing too many smart kids labeled ASD getting fixated on their autism. I think it would be healthier for the child to be fixated on art, writing, science, or some other special interest. Too many kids are becoming their label. When I was a student, I went to school with lots of socially awkward, geeky individuals. If DSM-5 guidelines were used, they would have been labeled autism spectrum disorder. If the ICD-11 had been used, they would have been placed in the mildest autism category, similar to the old Asperger's diagnosis.

Both fully verbal autism and more severe ASD often look the same in nonverbal or speech-delayed children under age five. When children labeled with ASD get older, they may diverge into two basic groups who need very different services. This highly divergent group is all assigned the same DSM-5 ASD label, and in poorly run programs, they are all given the same services. One group will continue to have a severe disability with either no speech or partial speech, and the other group will become fully verbal and capable of independent living and successful careers if they receive the right interventions. They usually are able to do grade-level or above-average schoolwork in at least one subject, such as reading or math.

There is a third subgroup in the nonverbal group who appear to have a severe intellectual disability. Examples of this type are Tito Mukhopadhyay and Naoki Higashida. Both of them can type independently, and they have good brains that are "locked in." From both an educational and functional standpoint, ASD becomes many different things in older children and adults. They may explain why there is so much controversy and differences of opinion in the autism community.

I am also concerned about children who should have an ASD label but they were given a label of oppositional defiant disorder (ODD) or disruptive mood dysregulation disorder (DMDD). In DMDD, the symptoms are frequent temper tantrums in a child older than six. The ODD label can be used for children of all ages. Its main symptoms are active defiance, vindictiveness, and sustained anger. Children who get these labels need to have firm limits placed on behavior and be given choices. For example, the choice could be doing homework before dinner or doing it after dinner. Choices help prevent the oppositional child from just saying "no."

Another effective way to reduce oppositional behavior is to challenge the child with doing a project that they could be really good at. Some examples may be building a more complicated LEGO structure or solving a more difficult math problem. Make sure you do not reward bad behavior. Sending a child to the principal's office to play with a tablet computer is rewarding.

In conclusion, parents and teachers must bust out of the ASD silo. DSM labels are not precise. They are behavioral profiles. Unfortunately, our system requires labels to get services. Remember to think about the specific services a child needs such as tutoring in reading, prevention of bullying, or social skills training for an older child or an intensive, early educational program for a nonverbal three-year-old.

References and Additional Reading

Aglinskas, A. et al. (2022) Contrastive machine learning reveals the structure of neuroanatomical variation in autism, *Science* 376(6597): 1070-1073.

American Psychiatric Association (2013) *Diagnostic and Statistical Manual of Mental Disorders* (DSM-5) Washington, D.C.: American Psychiatric Association.

Autism Europe (2018) World Health Organization updates classification of autism in the ICD-11 www.autism.europe.org (accessed June 21, 2019).

Baribeau, D.A. et al. (2019) Structural neuroimaging correlates of social deficits are similar in autism and attention-deficit/hyperactivity disorder: Analysis from the POND Network, *Translational Psychiatry*, 4(9):72doi:10.1038/s41398-019-0392-0.

Barnett, K. (2013) *The Spark: A Mother's Story of Nurturing, Genius and Autism*, Random House, New York NY.

Constantino, J.N. et al. (2003) Autistic traits in the general population: A twin study, *Archives of General Psychology*, 60:530-534.

Grandin, T., and Panek, R. (2013) *The Autistic Brain: Thinking Across the Spectrum*, Houghton Mifflin Harcourt, New York, NY.

Grzadzinski, R., Huerta, M. and Lord, C. (2013) DSM-5 and Autism Spectrum Disorders (ASDs): An Opportunity for Identifying Subgroups, *Molecular Autism*, 4:12-13. Doi:10.1186/2040-2392-4-12.

Hazen, E., McDougle, C., and Volkmar, F. (2013) Changes in the diagnostic criteria for autism in DSM-5 controversies and concerns, *The Journal of Clinical Psychiatry*, 74:739 doi:10.4088/JCP.13ac08550.

Higashida, N. and Mitchell, D. (2017) *Fall Down Seven Times and Get Up Eight: A Young Man's Voice from the Silence of Autism*, Random House, New York NY.

May, T. et al. (2018) Trends in the overlap of autism spectrum disorders and attention deficit hyperactivity disorder, prevalence, clinical management, language and genetics, *Current Disorder Reports*, 5:49-57.

Mukhopadhyay, T. (2008) *How Can I Talk if My Lips Don't Move: Inside My Autistic Mind*, Arcade Publishing, New York NY. Amazon Kindle and Barnes & Noble Nook available. Also available as audiobook from Amazon.

Pinto, R. (2015) The genetic overlap of attention-deficit/hyperactivity disorder and autistic-like traits: An investigation of individual symptom scales and cognitive markers, *Journal of Abnormal Child Psychology* doi:10.1007/s10802-015-0037-4.

Reed, G. M. et al. (2019) Innovations and changes in the ICD-11 classification of mental behavioral and neurodevelopmental disorder, *World Psychiatry*, 18 doi:10.1002/wps.20611.

Research in Autism (2019) Autism Spectrum Disorder, Diagnostic Criteria ICD-11, www.researchautism.net (Accessed January 25, 2019).

Sikela, J.M. and Sarles-Quick, V.B. (2018) Genomic tradeoffs: Are autism and schizophrenia the steep price for a human brain? *Human Genetics*, 137:1-13.

Traper, A. (2018) Discoveries in the genetics of ADHD in the 21st century: New findings and implications, *American Journal of Psychiatry*, 175:943-950.

World Health Organization (2019) ICD-11, Autism Spectrum Disorder, International Classifications of Diseases, World Health Organization, Geneva, Switzerland.

HIGH-QUALITY, BUDGET-FRIENDLY PROGRAMS FOR CHILDREN WITH ASD

I was lucky to get state-of-the-art early intervention (EI) and education while growing up in the early 1950s. Despite the lack of knowledge about autism and how to treat it (aside from institutionalization, which was the norm at that time), my mother had me in an excellent speech therapy nursery school by age three and I had a nanny who spent hours and hours per week playing turn-taking games and structured, enjoyable activities with me. In addition, our household's behavior rules were well-defined and social manners and social expectations were strictly enforced. Fortunately, my parents had enough money to pay for the programs that contributed to my development and laid the foundations for successful functioning as I grew up and ventured out on my own. Adjusting the fees for inflation, the cost of my program would probably be in the mid-range, compared to early intervention programs being used today. Many programs now available are much more expensive.

Can parents on a limited budget put together a good program for their young autistic child? The answer is yes, with a little thought and planning. I have talked to parents who have put together their own successful EI program after reading a few books and enlisting the help of volunteers. Self-motivation and an unfailing desire to help their child are needed as much as education about autism. The absolute worst thing a parent can do is to let their child sit and watch TV all day or zone out, unaware of his or her surroundings. This is precious time wasted, never to be regained.

CHAPTER 1: THE IMPORTANCE OF EARLY EDUCATIONAL INTERVENTION

Both research and practical experience have indicated that twenty or more hours of intense one-to-one interaction with an effective teacher and/or adult can kickstart speech and improve language and other behaviors in children with ASD. In many parts of the country a public school will provide only one or two hours a week of therapy with a speech therapist, an occupational therapist (OT), or a behavioral specialist. This is not enough to be really effective, but it does present an opportunity for training of the individuals who work with the child outside of the school day. This is especially true for parents, who need to take the lead and provide supplemental instruction themselves.

I recommend that parents in those situations approach the school therapists as "coaches" who can educate them about their child's autism and teach them how to do more intensive therapy at home. It also helps if family members or volunteers who are working with the child (for instance, a grandparent who has volunteered to work with a four year old) visit the school every week and watch the professional therapist work with the child. The professionals can give volunteers therapy assignments to work on with the child during the week. Invaluable information can be gleaned by watching sessions "in action" that no amount of reading will ever convey. Conversely, it might also be helpful from time to time to pay the therapist to spend an hour or two observing how the in-home program is unfolding. Sometimes a small change to a program can make a world of difference and it often takes a trained eye to spot situations like this. The weekly get-togethers are also a perfect time to discuss the child's progress and review goals and objectives for the coming week so everyone can keep track of progress and program changes.

Church and civic groups are a great place to find people who might be willing to work with a child. Other sources of help include students from the local high school or college students. When looking for volunteers to help teach the child, try to be specific about the types of things they will be doing. For instance, grandparents might feel comfortable volunteering to "play" with a child, or help provide "simple structured, repetitive drills"—those are familiar skills most people possess. Yet the same grandparent might feel ill-equipped if you ask her to "help out with the therapeutic behavior program designed for a child with autism." Most people don't know what that type of program entails, and they may think that only someone with a college degree would have relevant skills. Be sure to mention that you (or someone else) will be providing them with basic education and training on autism to further reinforce their ability to handle what comes up. Many people are genuinely interested in helping others, provided they get some training on how to do it.

I have observed that some teachers and therapists have a knack for working with children with ASD and others do not. Passive approaches do not work. Parents need to find the people, both professionals and nonprofessionals, who know how to be gently insistent, who keep the child motivated to learn, are child-centered in their approach, and are dedicated to teaching children with autism in a way they can learn, instead of insisting the child learn in the way they teach. Doing so naturally engages the child, which is the foundation of any effective program for children with autism, no matter what the cost. A useful book for learning teaching methods is *Autism Breakthrough* by Raun K. Kaufman.

Strategies that build on the child's areas of strength and appeals to their thinking patterns will be most effective.

DIFFERENT TYPES OF THINKING
IN AUTISM

R ecent studies on the brain, and especially on the brains of people diagnosed with autism spectrum disorders, are shedding light on the physiological underpinnings of our thoughts and emotions. We are gaining a better understanding of how neural pathways are formed and the extent to which biology influences behavior.

When I was much younger, I assumed that everybody perceived the world the same way I did. That is, that everybody thought in pictures. Early in my professional career, I got into a heated verbal argument with an engineer at a meat packing plant, and I told him he was stupid. He had designed a piece of equipment that had flaws that were obvious to me. My visual thinking gives me the ability to do a test run in my head on a piece of equipment I've designed, just like a virtual reality computer system. Mistakes can be found prior to construction when I do this. Now I realize his problem was not stupidity, it was a lack of visual thinking. It took me years to learn that the majority of people cannot do this and that visualization skills in some people are almost nonexistent.

All minds on the autism spectrum are detail-oriented, but how they specialize varies. By questioning many people, both on and off the spectrum, I have learned that there are three different types of specialized thinking with crossover among these specialized thinking patterns. Determining thinking types in three year old children is often not possible. Dominant thinking types usually become more obvious when a child is seven to nine:

- Visual thinkers think in photorealistic pictures, like me (object visualizers).
- Music and math patterned thinkers (visual-spatial).
- Verbal thinkers (not visual thinkers).

Since autism is so variable, there may be mixtures of the different types. For instance, a child may have strong music/math patterned thinking, but also have good visual thinking abilities. Or a verbal thinker may also have good math or foreign language skills. The importance of understanding these three ways of thinking comes into play when trying to teach children with ASD. Strategies that build on the child's area of strength and appeal to their thinking patterns will be most effective. This is most likely to become evident between the ages of five and eight. It is often difficult to identify the strengths of children younger than five, unless savant skills are unfolding. In a study of college students, the major they chose was partially determined by their cognitive style. Students in three different majors were assessed. Engineering students preferred visual-spatial pattern thinking. Fine arts and psychology students preferred visual thinking (object visualizers) and verbal thinking was only prominent in psychology students.

Visual Thinkers (Object Visualizers)

These children often love art and building blocks, such as Legos®, and they will often produce beautiful drawings. They get easily immersed in projects that have a tangible, hands-on opportunity for learning. Math concepts, such as adding and subtracting, need to be taught starting with concrete objects the child can touch. Drawing and other art skills should be encouraged. These kids may have a really difficult time with algebra. They should be moved immediately ahead into geometry because geometry is more visual. If a child only draws one thing, such as airplanes, encourage him/her to draw other related objects, such as the airport runways, or the hangars, or cars going to the airport. Broadening a child's emerging skills helps him/her be more flexible in his/her thinking patterns. Keep in mind that because the child's "native language" is pictures, verbal responses can take longer to form. Each request has to be translated from words to pictures before it can be processed, and then the response needs to be translated from pictures into words before it is spoken. Visual thinkers often have difficulty doing algebra because of its abstract nature, but some can do geometry and trigonometry quite easily. Visual thinkers often find success in careers as artists, graphic designers, photographers, or industrial engineers. Another field visual thinkers like me can excel in is skilled trades. Visual thinkers who were at one time addicted to video games have gone into successful careers in auto mechanics. They ultimately discovered that engines were more interesting than video games.

There is a huge shortage of plumbers, electricians, mechanics, and welders who can read blueprints. One of the worst things some schools have done was removing vocational classes. These are good careers that will never get replaced by artificial intelligence or computers.

Music and Math Thinkers (Visual-Spatial)

Patterns instead of pictures dominate the thinking processes of these children. Both music and math are a world of patterns, and children who think this way can have strong associative abilities. Research shows that they have superior abilities to perform mental rotation tasks. They like finding relationships between numbers or musical notes. Some children may have savant-type calculation skills or are able to play a piece of music after hearing it just once. Musical talent often emerges without formal instruction. Many of these children can teach themselves if instruments are available. When they grow up, pattern thinkers are often very good at computer programming, engineering, or music. Some of these children should be advanced several grades ahead in math, depending on their abilities, but they may need special education in reading, which may lag behind. Many of these kids can easily do math in their heads. They should be allowed to do this. They are likely to get bored in a math class that is too easy. They also need to be exposed to computer programming and coding. One way to determine how a child thinks is to expose him/her to both algebra and geometry books.

Verbal Thinkers

These children love lists and numbers. Often, they will memorize bus timetables and events in history. Interest areas often include history, geography, weather, and sports statistics. They are not visual thinkers. Parents and teachers can use these interests and talents as motivators for learning the less interesting parts of academics. Some verbal thinkers are whizzes at learning many different foreign languages. I know individuals with verbal thinking skills who have been successfully employed in sales of specialized products such as cars, stage acting, accounting, factual/technical writing, and pharmacology. These are all areas where memorization of many facts is a talent that other people will appreciate.

The thinking patterns of individuals with ASD are markedly different from the way "normal" people think. Because of this, too much emphasis is placed on what they "can't do," and opportunities to capitalize on their different but often creative and novel ways of thinking fall by the wayside. An interesting new study showed that many students with autism who attend college enroll in STEM fields such as computer science or engineering. While impairments and challenges to exist, greater progress can be made teaching these individuals when parents and teachers work on building the child's strengths and teach in a manner aligned with their basic pattern of thinking.

References and Additional Reading

Blazhenkova, O. et al. (2011) Object-spatial imagery and verbal cognitive styles in children and adolescents: Developmental trajectories in relation to ability, Learning and Individual Differences.

Chiang, H.M. and Lin, Y.H. (2007) Mathematical ability of students with Asperger syndrome and high-functioning autism, *Autism* 11:547-556.

Grandin, T. (2009) How does visual thinking work in the mind of a person with autism" A personal account. Physiological Transactions of the Royal Society, London, UYK, 364:1437-1442.

Grandin, T. and Lerner, B. (2022) *Visual Thinking: The Hidden Gifts of People Who Think in Pictures, Patterns and Abstractions*. Riverhead Books, Penguin Random House, New York, NY.

Grandin, T. and Panek, R. (2013) *The Autistic Brain*, Houghton Mifflin Harcourt, New York, NY.

Hegarty, M., and Kozhevnikov, M. (1999) Types of visual-spatial representations and mathematical problem solving, *Journal of Educational Psychology*, 91:684-689.

Hoffner, T.N. (2016) More evidence for three kinds of cognitive styles: Validating the object-spatial imagery and verbal questionnaire using eye tracking when learning with texts and pictures, *Applied Cognitive Psyhology* 31(1) doi. org/10.1002/acp.3300.

Jones, C.R.G. et al. (2009) Reading and arithmetic in adolescents with autism spectrum disorders: Peaks and dips in attainment, *Neuropsychology*, 23:718-728.

Kozhevnikov, M. and Blazenkova, O. (2013) Individual differences in object versus spatial imagery: From neural correlates to real world applications, In: S. Lacey and R. Lawson (Editors), *Multisensory Imagery*, 229-308.

Kochevnikov, M. et al. (2002) Revising the visualizer—Verbal dimension: Evidence for two types of visualizers, *Cognition and Instruction*, 20:47-77.

Mazard, A. et al (2004) A PET meta-analysis of object and spatial mental imagery, *European Journal of Cognitive Psychology* 16:673-695.

Perez-Fabello, M.J. et al. (2018) Object spatial imagery in fine arts, psychology and engineering, *Thinking Skills and Creativity* 27:131-138.

Shonulsky, S.et al. (2019) STEM faculty experiences teaching students with autism, *Journal of STEM Teacher Education* 53(2) Article 4.

Resources for Computer Coding for Kids

scratch.mit.edu

sphero.com

code.org

codakid

khanacademy.org

Codecademy

childhood101.com

coderkids.com

Stevenson, J.L. and Gernsbacher, M.A. (2013) Abstract spatial reasoning as an autistic strength. *PLOS ONE* doi:10.1371/journal.pone.0059329.

McGrath, J. et al. (2012) Atypical visual spatial processing in autism: Insight from functional connectivity analysis, *Autism Research*, 5:314-330.

Soulieres, I. et al., (2011) The level and nature of autistic intelligence II: What about Asperger syndrome? *PLOS One*. Doi:10.1371/journal.pone.0025372.

HIGHER EXPECTATIONS YIELD RESULTS

Young children with autism spectrum disorders do not learn by listening to and watching others, as do typical children. They need to be specifically taught things that others seem to learn by osmosis. A good teacher is gently insistent with a young autistic child in order to get progress. The teacher has to be careful not to cause sensory overload, but at the same time has to be somewhat intrusive into the child's world of stimming or silent withdrawal in order for the child to engage in learning.

When children get a little older, they need to be exposed to many different things to stimulate their continued learning in different areas of life. There also need to be expectations for proper social behavior. When I look back at my life, my mother made me do a number of things I did not like, but these activities were really beneficial. They gave me opportunities to practice social skills, converse with less familiar people, develop self-esteem and learn to negotiate unanticipated changes. None of these activities caused major problems with sensory overload. While Mother may have pushed me to do things, she understood well that a child should never be forced into a situation that includes painful sensory stimulation.

By age five, I was required to dress up and behave in church and sit through formal dinners both at home and at Granny's. When I didn't, there was a consequence, and I lost a privilege that meant something to me. Fortunately, our church had a beautiful old-fashioned organ I liked. Most of the service was boring to me, but that organ made it somewhat tolerable to sit through. A modern church with loud, amplified music probably would be sensory overload to someone like me.

For me, certain loud sounds, such as the school bell, were like a dentist drill hitting a nerve. Sometimes a child can be desensitized to a sound if the

28

child can control that sound. The bell may be better tolerated if the child is allowed to turn it on and off after school hours. One child who feared the vacuum cleaner learned to love it when he could control the sound by turning it on and off. High expectations are important, but some adjustments may be necessary to prevent sensory overload.

During my elementary school years, Mother had me be her party hostess. I had to greet each guest and serve them snacks. This taught me important social skills, and it made me feel proud to be participating in their "grown-up" event. It also provided the opportunity to learn how to talk to many different people.

When I was reluctant to learn to ride a bike, I was urged to learn. Mother was always testing the limits on how far she could push me. I became motivated to learn after I missed a bike trip to the Coca Cola plant.

When I was a teenager, the opportunity arose for me to visit my aunt's ranch in Arizona. At the time, I was having non-stop panic attacks and was afraid to go. Mother gave me the choice to go for two weeks or the whole summer. When I got there, I loved it and stayed all summer. Aunt Ann became one of my important mentors. My career in livestock equipment design would have never started if I had been allowed to stay home.

I often needed a certain amount of pushing to do new things by myself. I was good at building things, but afraid to go to the lumber yard and buy the wood by myself. Mother made me do it. She never let my autism be an excuse for not trying something she knew would be beneficial for me to learn. I came back crying from that outing, but I had the wood with me. Further trips to the lumber yard were easy. At one of my early jobs my boss made me "cold call" cattle magazines to get articles published. After I got over the initial fear, I found I was good at getting articles into national cattle publications. In all of the above cases, either my mother or a boss had to push me to do things even though I was afraid. Yet the things I learned—especially about myself—were priceless.

After I started my freelance design business, I almost gave it up because an early client was not 100 percent satisfied. My black and white thinking led me to believe that clients would always be 100 percent satisfied. Fortunately, my good friend Jim Uhl, the contractor who built my systems, would not let me quit. He actively kept pushing and talking to me and asking for the next drawing. When I produced a new drawing, he praised it. Now I know that 100 percent client satisfaction is impossible. My life and career could have been derailed and wrecked if my mother and business associates had not pushed me to do things. Mother did not let me lie around the house, and never viewed my autism as rendering me incapable. Business associates stayed after me and made me do things. These adult mentors are a grown-up version of a good special education teacher who is gently insistent with a three-year-old child with autism. What it demonstrates overall is that people with ASD can learn and succeed when others around them believe in their abilities and hold high expectations of them.

To summarize this chapter, parents and teachers need to "stretch" individuals on the autism spectrum. They need to be stretched just outside their comfort zone for them to develop. However, there must be no sudden surprises, because surprises are frightening. I am seeing too many individuals with ASD who have not learned basic skills, such as shopping and shaking hands. At conferences, I see parents speaking for their child when their child should be speaking for himself. They are being overprotected and sheltered too much. It made me really happy when I encouraged a child with ASD to ask her own question in front of a whole lot of people at a conference. When the child was successful speaking in front of the crowd, the audience clapped.

TEACHING TURN TAKING AND THE

ABILITY TO WAIT

I visited a school in Australia that was using simple, innovative methods to teach turn taking and the ability to wait. Diane Heaney, the direc- tor of education for the AEIOU Foundation for Children with Autism, explained the concept of this early educational program. When designing this program, she asked the question, "What are the most important things to teach children to get them ready for a mainstream first-grade class?" They are the ability to talk, take turns, sit still, exhibit good table manners, use the toilet independently, and have social engagement.

The children in her program start at age two to three years and are all non- verbal or have obviously delayed verbal skills. At the end of the three-year program, approximately 75 percent of the children have gained enough skills to go to a mainstream school. Some may need an aide or other support. The school is a full-day program, and the kids go home in the afternoon. The staff- to-student ratio is one to two.

When the children first arrive in her program, they get standard applied behavior analysis (ABA) to get language started.

After verbal skills develop, they move away from one-on-one ABA to activities that teach turn taking and the ability to wait.

Teaching Turn Taking

They use three different methods to teach turn taking: playing traditional board games, projecting an educational video game on a Smartboard, and sharing a tablet computer (iPad). I loved the projected video game. They used a Curious George counting game that has very distinct activities where each turn is independent (i.e., doesn't depend on the previous child's answer). Because the game is projected on a Smartboard, when each child takes his turn, the other children have to sit and watch. The Smartboard responds like a gigantic touch screen iPad. The key is having the children who wait be able to watch the child who is taking his turn to perform. This activity teaches both turn taking and sitting quietly on a chair. The projected image on the Smartboard prevents fighting over a physical tablet computer.

The following procedure is used by the teacher:

Step 1: A single child learns to play the game by himself for a few minutes and finds it rewarding.

Step 2: Two children take turns, one at a time, walking to the Smartboard and touching the screen to play a single turn of the game. The child who is waiting to take his turn must remain in his chair.

Step 3: When two children can wait and take turns, a child on a third chair is added.

Step 4: When three children can wait and take turns, a fourth child on a fourth chair is added.

If a Smartboard is not available, a tablet should be placed on a table in front of the children and each child would have to walk up and take his turn and then go back to his chair. The tablet should be positioned so that the children who are waiting can see the screen. The tablet may need to be attached to a sturdy stand so a child cannot pick it up and try to take it back to his chair. The principle is to teach the children to inhibit a response in order to get a reward. To make it easier for the other children who are waiting to watch what is happening on the tablet, the screen image could be easily projected on the wall with a standard LCD projector.

The children also have to learn how to take turns while playing traditional board games and passing a smartphone or tablet from one child to another. Teaching the children to share a phone or tablet they can hold may be more difficult. The previously described activity should be mastered first.

Remember, all school activities involving electronics with children under the age of five should always be done as an interactive activity under the supervision of a teacher. Solitary play on electronic devices must be avoided. When electronics are used, children must be interacting with either other children or an adult.

Further Reading

Danesh, A.A. et al. (2021) Hyperacusis in autism spectrum disorders, *Audiology Research*, 11: 547-556.

Grandin, T. and Panek, R. (2013) *The Autistic Brain*, Houghton Mifflin Harcourt, New York, NY.

Van de Boogert, F. et al. (2021) Sensory processing and aggressive behavior in adults with autism spectrum disorders, *Brain Science*, 11(1). 96.

WHAT SCHOOL IS BEST FOR MY CHILD WITH ASD?

I get asked all the time by parents about which school is the best for their child with autism. I have observed that success in school depends so much on the particular school and the people who are involved. Public or private is not an issue. It depends on the particular staff who work with your child. It is really important for PreK and elementary school children to get lots of contact with neurotypical children to learn appropriate social behavior.

There are many children with autism or other labels who do really well in their local public school system and are mainstreamed in a regular classroom. Children who have been successfully mainstreamed range from fully verbal advanced placement (AP) students to students who are nonverbal and/or are more severely involved. Unfortunately, there are other schools that are doing poorly due to a variety of factors.

Some parents choose to homeschool their child. There are lots of good homeschooling materials on the Internet, such as Khan Academy (www.khanacademy.org), which offers a multitude of free classroom materials for math and science. Others look for a special school for their spectrum kid.

Special Schools for ASD

Recently I toured specialized schools for both elementary and high school students who are on the spectrum. Within the last few years, many new specialized schools have opened. They tend to fall into two types. One is designed for fully verbal children who have autism, attention deficit hyperactivity disorder

(ADHD), dyslexia, or some other learning problem. The kids are enrolled in their new school to get away from being bullied or to keep from becoming lost in the crowd in a huge school. The other type of special school is designed to fit the needs of students who are nonverbal and/or have challenging behaviors.

I have visited several schools that enroll children with autism or other labels who just do not fit in at a regular school. Teasing and bullying were often a major reason for leaving the former school. Problems with aggression in many students on the spectrum disappeared when the teasing stopped. None of these schools accepted kids who had been in serious trouble with the law. Most of the students I met at these schools were fully verbal and did not have serious problems, such as self-injurious behavior. They were kids who were a lot like me when I was their age. The student population ranged from 30 to 150.

Keeping the schools small is one of the keys to their success.

Effective Classrooms for ASD

I observed two types of classrooms at these specialized schools. The first type was just like my old 1950s–style elementary school. There were about 12 children in each class, and they all sat at desks while the teacher taught in the front of the classroom.

Keeping classes small was essential. The school enrolled about 100 students, ranging from kindergarten through high school. These students were mainly the socially awkward geeky kids who got picked on by bullies. I talked to them at an assembly where all the students sat on the floor of the gym, and their behavior was wonderful!

The other type of classroom I observed had a teacher to student ratio of 1:3 or 1:4. Students from several different grades were in the same classroom, and students were taught in subject areas such as math, science, or English. Each student worked at his own pace as the teacher rotated among the students. In all the classrooms a quiet environment was maintained because many students had difficulty with sensory issues. I was glad to see that in most of the classrooms hands-on activities were used.

Every child is different. What works for one may not work for another. There is also a lot of variation in schools, from city to city, and region to region. You know your child best. Take into account your child's strengths and challenges when deciding the right school for him to find the best possible match. Most importantly, make sure the staff at the school have the proper training and background and use instructional methods that are a good fit for your child's needs.

CHAPTER   TWO

TEACHING & EDUCATION

Good teachers understand that for a child to learn, the teaching style must match the student's learning style.

E very child with ASD has his or her own personality and profile of strengths and weaknesses; this is no different than with typical children. They can be introverts or extroverts, have a sunny disposition or be cranky, love music or math. Parents and educators can easily forget this, and attribute every action or reaction of the child to autism, and therefore in need of dissection and "fixing." The goal in teaching children with autism is not to turn them into clones of their typical peers (i.e., "normal"). When you think about it, not all characteristics exhibited by typical people are worthy of being modeled. A much more meaningful perspective is to teach this population the academic and interpersonal skills they need to be functional in the world and use their talents to the best of their ability.

Autism is not a death sentence for a child or the family. It brings with it great challenges, but it can also bring to the child the seeds of great talents and unique abilities. It is the responsibility of parents and educators to find those seeds, nurture them, and make sure they grow. That should be the goal of teaching and education for children with ASD too, not just for neuromajority children.

The different thinking patterns of individuals with autism require parents and educators to teach from a new frame of reference, one aligned with their autism way of thinking. Expecting children with ASD to learn via the conventional curriculum and teaching methods that "have always worked" for typical children is to set everyone up for failure right from the start. It would be like placing a young child on a grown up's chair and expecting his feet to reach the floor. That's just silly, isn't it? Yet, surprisingly, that is still how many schools and educators approach students with ASD. Good teachers understand that for a child to learn, the teaching style must match the student's learning style. With autism it is not enough to match the teaching style to the child's learning type.

Educators must take this idea one step further, and be continuously mindful that students with ASD come to school without a developed social thinking framework. This is the aspect of ASD that can be difficult for adults to understand, envision, and work around. Our public education system is built upon the premise that children enter school with basic social functioning skills in place. Kids with autism—with their characteristic social thinking challenges—enter school already lagging far behind their classmates. Teachers who don't recognize this and don't make accommodations to teach social thinking and social skills alongside traditional academics just further limit the opportunities children with ASD have to learn and grow.

Education works best when both parents and teachers work together as a team. When I was in elementary school, the rules were the same at home and school. If I had a tantrum at either home or school, the rule was no television for one night. Tantrums caused by loud noise or sensory overload did not have a penalty. Some children may need to take sensory breaks to calm down. An occupational therapist who is skilled in autistic sensory problems should be consulted.

To Mainstream or Not to Mainstream?

At age five I started attending a small school with neuromajority children. In today's language, that would be called mainstreaming. It is important to note that this worked for me because the structure and composition of the class was well matched to my needs. The school had highly structured old-fashioned classes with only twelve students.

Children were expected to behave and there were strict rules, enforced consistently, and with consequences applied for infractions. The environment was relatively quiet and controlled, without a high degree of sensory stimulation. In this environment I did not need an aide. Contrast that classroom with today's learning environment. In a class of thirty students, with a single teacher, in a less structured classroom within a larger school, I would never have survived without the direct assistance of a one-on-one aide.

Whether or not to mainstream an elementary school child on the autism spectrum is a decision that should take many factors into consideration. After countless discussions with parents and teachers, I have come to the conclusion that much depends on the particular school and the particular teachers in that school. The idea of mainstreaming is a worthy goal, and in an ideal situation—where all the variables are working in favor of the child with ASD—it can be a highly positive experience. But the reality of the situation is often the opposite: lack of teacher training, large classes, limited opportunities for individual modifications, and lack of funding to support one-on-one paraprofessionals can render this environment disastrous for the spectrum child.

For elementary school children on the fully verbal end of the autism spectrum, I usually favor mainstreaming because it is essential for them to learn social skills from typically developing children. If a child is homeschooled or goes to a special school, it is imperative that the child has regular engagement with typical peers. For nonverbal children, mainstreaming works well in some situations—again, much depends on the school, its expertise in autism, and its program. A special school may be a better choice for the nonverbal or cognitively impaired child with autism, especially in cases where severe, disruptive behavior problems exist and need to be addressed.

Parents frequently ask me whether or not they should change the school or program their child is in. My response is to ask this question: "Is your child making progress and improving where he is now?" If they say he is, I usually recommend staying in the school or the program and then discuss whether some additional services or program modifications may be needed.

For instance, the child may do even better with more attention to physical exercise, or addressing his sensory problems, or adding a few more hours of individualized ABA therapy or social skills training.

However, if the child is making little or no progress, and the school's attitude is not supportive or accommodating of the different needs and learning styles of children with ASD so the parent is constantly battling for even the most basic services, it may be best to find a different school or program. This will, of course, require time and effort on the part of the parent, but it is important for parents to keep the end goal in sight—giving the child as much opportunity to learn and acquire needed skills in as supportive an environment as possible.

It does no one good, and least of all the child, for a parent to repeatedly fight a school system, either within Individualized Education Plan (IEP) meetings or through due process, to win their case within an environment of individuals who are not interested in truly helping the child.

Sadly, this scenario plays out in schools and districts across the country. Valuable time that could be spent in meaningful instruction that helps the child is wasted while the school and parent butt heads for not just months, but in many cases, years. The child—and the child's needs—should always remain the focus. If the school is not child-focused, then parents should find one that is.

I reiterate a point made earlier: so much depends on the particular people working with the child. In one case, a third grader in a good school with an excellent reputation had several teachers who simply did not like him, nor did they attempt to understand his learning style and modify instruction to meet that style. The child hated going to school. I suggested the parents try to find a different school. They did, and the child is now doing great in his new school. In my conversations with parents and teachers, I have also observed that it doesn't matter whether the elementary school is public or private; this is seldom the issue. More depends on local conditions: the school's perception of children with disabilities and philosophy towards their education, the extent to which staff have been trained, and receive ongoing training on autism spectrum disorders and how best to work with this population, and the support provided by administration to staff in educating these students. Decisions must be made on a case-by-case basis.

The Parent Guilt Trip

It is unfortunate, but a reality of today's society, that some individuals and companies who run special schools, sell therapy services, or market products to the autism community often try to put parents on a guilt trip. All parents want what's best for their child, and parents of newly diagnosed children can be especially vulnerable. These vendors prey upon parents' emotions in advertising and personal encounters, suggesting that parents are not good parents if they don't try their program or product, or that by not using whatever it is they offer, the parent isn't doing "everything possible" to help their child. Some go as far as to tell parents that their child is doomed unless they use their program or product.

One parent called me about a situation just like this. The family was ready to sell their house to have the funds needed to send their four year old child with autism to a special school in another state. I asked him if the child was learning and making progress at the local public school. The dad told me he was. Yet, the special school was making great claims about the progress their child would make with them. I talked with the dad about the negative impact disrupting the child's life like this might have, taking him away from his family and familiar surroundings, and sending him to a school in another state. The very real possibility existed that the child could get worse, rather than better. By the time we ended our conversation, the parents decided to keep their child in his local school and supplement his education with some additional hours of one-to-one therapy.

The articles in this section shed light on the different thinking and learning patterns of children with ASD. They offer many teaching tips to help children succeed. Among the different topics covered are areas that I view as especially important: developing the child's strengths, using a child's obsessions to motivate schoolwork, and teaching the child problem-solving and thinking skills that will assist him not just during his limited years in school, but throughout his entire life.

When I was a child in the 1950s, manners and social skills were taught to all children in a more structured and systematic manner. This was extremely helpful for me and for many people of my generation who were on the milder end of the autism spectrum. When I was in college, I had several friends who today would have been labeled with autism. My friends who were raised much like I was, acquired and retained good jobs. Most individuals on the spectrum have areas of strength that can be nurtured and developed into marketable employment skills.

Parents in the 1950s constantly used "teachable moments" to teach manners. Every day there will be many teachable moments. The big mistake many parents and teachers make when a child does something wrong is to scream "No." A better technique is to give the instruction instead. For example, if the child eats mashed potatoes with his hands say, "Use the fork." If I forgot to say "please" or "thank you," mother would cue me and say, "You forgot to say   and wait for me to respond." If I touched items in a store, she would say, "Put it back. You only touch things you will be buying." You always give instructions on how to behave.

Books That Give Insight into Autistic Thinking & Learning Patterns

Grandin, T. (2005). *Unwritten Rules of Social Relationships: Decoding Social Mysteries Through the Unique Perspectives of Autism.* Arlington, TX: Future Horizons, Inc.

Grandin T. (2006). *Thinking in Pictures* (Expanded Edition). New York: Vintage Press/Random House.

Tammet D. (2007). *Born on a Blue Day: Inside the Extraordinary Mind of an Autistic Savant.* New York: Free Press.

Grandin, T. and Panek , R. (2013). *The Autistic Brain.* Houghton Mifflin Harcourt, New York, NY.

FINDING A CHILD'S AREA OF STRENGTH

I n one of my 2005 columns in the *Autism Asperger's Digest*, I discussed the three different types of specialized thinking in individuals with high functioning autism. Children on the spectrum usually have an area of strength and an area of deficit. Many parents and teachers have asked me, "How do you determine the child's area of strength?" A child usually has to be at least in elementary school before it becomes evident. In many cases, the area of strength cannot be determined in a child younger than five years old. In some cases the area of strength doesn't emerge until some of the other, more dominant sensory or behavioral issues have been remediated.

The first type is the visual thinkers, who think in photorealistic pictures. I am in this category, and my mind works like Google Images. When I was in elementary school, my visual thinking skills were expressed in art and drawing. Children who are visual thinkers will usually produce many beautiful drawings by the time they are in third or fourth grade. In my career, I use my visual thinking skills to design livestock-handling facilities. Visual thinkers often go into such careers as graphic arts, industrial design, or architecture.

The second type is the pattern thinkers, who are often very good at math and music. They see relationships and patterns between numbers and sounds. In elementary school, some of these children will play a musical instrument really well. Others will be good at both music and math, and another group will be math lovers with no musical interest. It is important to challenge these kids with advanced math. If they are forced to do "baby" math, they will get bored. If an elementary school student can do high school math, he or she should be encouraged to study it. Both photorealistic visual thinkers and pattern thinkers often excel at building structures with blocks and Legos®. Pattern

46

thinkers can have successful careers as engineers, computer programmers or musicians. However, the pattern thinkers will often need some extra help with reading and writing composition.

The third type is the verbal thinker. These children are word specialists, and they know all the facts about their favorite subjects. For many of these kids, history is their favorite subject, and their writing skills are good. The word thinkers are not visual thinkers, and they will usually have little interest in art, drawing, or Legos®. Individuals who are word specialists are often really good at journalism, being speech therapists, and any job that requires careful record keeping.

Build Up Strengths

Too often educators pound away at the deficits and neglect to build up the child's area of strength. Most visual thinkers and some pattern thinkers cannot do algebra. Algebra was impossible for me, and so I was never allowed to try geometry or trigonometry. Endless hours of algebra drills were useless. I did not understand it because there was nothing to visualize. When I discuss this at conferences, I find many children and adults on the spectrum who failed algebra but were able to do geometry and trigonometry. They should be allowed to substitute these higher maths for algebra. Algebra is NOT a prerequisite for geometry and trigonometry for some types of brains.

Educators need to understand that these individuals think differently and that what works for the typical-minded student may not work for the spectrum individual. I got through college math because in the '60s, algebra had been replaced with finite math, where I studied probability and matrices. It was difficult, but with tutoring I was able to do it. Finite math had things I could visualize. If I had been forced to take college algebra, I would have failed college math. Students should be allowed to substitute any higher math for algebra. One mother told me her son got straight As in college physics but he could not graduate from high school because he failed algebra.

One of the worst things many schools have done is removing classes such as art, sewing, band, auto repair, welding, music, theater, and other "hands on" classes. In elementary school, I would have been lost without art, sewing, and woodworking class. These were the classes where I had strengths and I learned skills that became the basis of my work on design and livestock facilities.

In conclusion, focusing only on the deficits of individuals with autism does nothing to prepare them for the real world that lies outside of school. Most individuals on the spectrum have areas of strength that can be nurtured and developed into marketable employment skills. Teachers and parents need to build on these areas of strength starting when the child is young and continue through middle and high school. In so doing, we provide these individuals with the opportunity to have satisfying careers they can enjoy for the rest of their lives.

Teachers and parents need to help both children and adults with autism take all the little details they have in their head and put them into categories to form concepts and promote generalization.

TEACHING HOW TO GENERALIZE

Many children and people with autism are not able to take all the facts they know and link them together to form concepts. What has worked for me is to use my visual thinking to form concepts and categories. Explaining how I do this may help parents and professionals teach children with autism how to form concepts and generalizations.

When I was a little child, I knew that cats and dogs were different because dogs were bigger than cats. When the neighbors bought a little Dachshund, I could no longer categorize dogs by size. Rosie the Dachshund was the same size as a cat. I can remember looking intently at Rosie to find some visual characteristic that both our Golden Retriever and Rosie had in common.

I noticed that all dogs, regardless of size, had the same kind of nose. Therefore, dogs could be placed in a separate category from cats because there are certain physical features that every dog has that no cat has.

Dogs and cats can also be differentiated by the sounds they make and their different smells. My brain puts specific examples into categories like a spreadsheet. The ability to form categories will improve as I put more specific examples into my database.

Categorizing things can be taught. Kindergarten children learn to categorize all the red objects or all the square objects. Irene Pepperberg, a scientist at the University of Arizona, taught her parrot, Alex, to differentiate and identify objects by color and shape. He could pick out all the red square blocks from a tray containing red balls, blue square blocks, and red blocks. He understood categorization of objects by color, shape, and size. Teaching children and adults with autism to categorize and form concepts starts first with teaching simple categories such as color and shape. From this, we can help them understand that certain facts they have memorized can be placed in one category and other facts can be placed in another category.

Teaching Concepts Such as Danger

Many parents have asked me, "How do I teach my child not to run into the street?" or "He knows not to run into the street at our house, but at Grandma's he runs into the street." In the first situation, the child actually has no concept of danger at all; in the second, he is not able to generalize what he has learned at home to a new house and street.

Danger as a concept is too abstract for the mind of a person who thinks in pictures. I did not understand that being hit by a car would be dangerous until I saw a squashed squirrel in the road and my nanny told me that it had been run over by a car. Unlike the cartoon characters on TV, the squirrel did not survive. I then understood the cause and effect of being run over.

After the squirrel incident, how did I learn that all cars on all streets are dangerous? It is just like learning concepts like the color red or square versus round. I had to learn that no matter where I was located, all cars and all streets had certain common features. When I was a child, safety concepts were drilled into my head with a book of safety songs. I sang about always looking both ways before crossing a street to make sure a car was not coming. To help me generalize, my nanny took my sister and me for walks around the neighborhood. On many different streets she had me look both ways before crossing. This is the same way that guide dogs for the blind are trained. The dog must be able to recognize stop lights, intersections, and streets in a strange place. During training, he is taken to many different streets. He then has visual, auditory and olfactory (smell) memories of many different streets. From these memories, the dog is able to recognize a street in a strange place.

For either the guide dog or the person with autism to understand the concept of "street," they have to see more than one street. Autistic thinking is specific as opposed to general. To learn a concept of "dog" or "street," I had to see many specific dogs or streets before the general concept could be formed. A general concept such as a street—without pictures of many specific streets stored in my memory bank—is absolutely meaningless.

Autistic thinking is always detailed and specific. Teachers and parents need to help both children and adults with autism take all the little details they have in their head and put them into categories to form concepts and promote generalization.

Interests and talents can turn into careers.

THE IMPORTANCE OF DEVELOPING TALENT

There is often too much emphasis in the world of autism on the deficits of these children and not enough emphasis on developing the special talents that many of them possess. Talents need to be developed because they can form the basis of skills that will make a person with autism employable.

Abilities such as drawing or math skills need to be nurtured and expanded. The abilities may not become fully apparent until the child is seven or eight. If a child likes to draw trains, that interest should be broadened into other activities, such as reading a book about trains or doing a math problem calculating the time it would take to travel from Boston to Chicago.

It is a mistake to stamp out a child's special interests, however odd they may seem at the time. In my own case, my talent in art was encouraged. My mother bought me professional art materials and a book on perspective drawing when I was in grade school.

Fixations and special interests should be directed into constructive channels instead of being abolished to make a person more "normal." The career I have today as a designer of livestock facilities is based on my talent areas. I use my visual thinking to design equipment. As a teenager, I became fixated on cattle squeeze chutes after I discovered that when I got in a cattle squeeze chute it relieved my anxiety. Fixations can be great motivators if they are properly channeled. My high school teacher directed my interest in cattle chutes into motivating me to study science and to study more in school. He told me that if I learned more about the field of sensory perception, I could find out why the pressure applied by the cattle chute was relaxing. Now, instead of boring everybody I knew with endless talk about cattle chutes, I immersed myself in the study of science. My original interest in the cattle chute also led to an interest in the behavior of cattle, then the design of systems, which led to the development of my career.

This is an example of taking a fixation and broadening it out into something constructive. Sometimes teachers and parents put so much emphasis on making a teenager more social that developing talents is neglected. Teaching social skills is very important, but if the person with autism is stripped of all their special interests, they may lose meaning in their life. "I am what I think and do, more than what I feel." Social interactions can be developed through shared interests. I had friends as a child because other children liked making craft projects with me.

During the difficult years of high school, special interest clubs can be a lifesaver.

Recently I watched a TV documentary about autism. One of the people profiled liked to raise chickens. Her life took on meaning when she discovered that other people shared the same hobby. When she joined a poultry hobby club, she received social recognition for being an expert. Interests and talents can turn into careers. Developing and nurturing these unique abilities can make life more fulfilling for a person with autism.

TEACHING PEOPLE ON THE AUTISM SPECTRUM TO BE MORE FLEXIBLE

Rigidity in both behavior and thinking is a major characteristic of people with autism and Asperger's. They have difficulty understanding the concept that sometimes it is okay to break a rule. I heard about a case where an autistic boy had a severe injury but he did not leave the school bus stop to get help.

He had been taught to stay at the bus stop so that he would not miss the bus; he could not break that rule. Common sense would have told most people that getting help for a severe injury would be more important than missing the bus. But not to this young man.

How can common sense be taught? I think it starts with teaching flexible thinking at a young age. Structure is good for children with autism, but sometimes plans can, and need to be, changed. When I was little, my nanny made my sister and me do a variety of activities. This variety prevented rigid behavior patterns from forming. I became more accustomed to changes in our daily or weekly routines and learned that I could still manage when change occurred. This same principle applies to animals. Cattle that are always fed from the red truck by Jim may panic if Sally pulls up in a white truck to feed them. To prevent this problem, progressive ranchers have learned to alter routines slightly so that cattle learn to accept some variation.

Another way to teach flexible thinking is to use visual metaphors, such as mixing paint. To understand complex situations, such as when occasionally a good friend does something nasty, I imagine mixing white and black paint. If the friend's behavior is mostly nice, the mixture is a very light gray; if the person is really not a friend then the mixture is a very dark gray. Black-and-white thinking on concepts such as "good" and "bad" can be a problem. There are degrees of badness that can be ranked in categories by severity, i.e., 1) stealing a pen, 2) punching another person, 3) robbing a bank, and 4) murder.

Flexibility can also be taught by showing the person with autism that categories can change. Objects can be sorted by color, function, or material. To test this idea, I grabbed a bunch of black, red, and yellow objects in my office and laid them on the floor. They were a stapler, a roll of tape, a ball, videotapes, a toolbox, a hat, and pens. Depending upon the situation, any of these objects could be used for either work or play. Ask the child to give concrete examples of using a stapler for work or play. For instance, stapling office papers is work; stapling a kite together is play. Simple situations like this that teach a child flexibility in thinking and relating can be found numerous times in each day.

Children do need to be taught that some rules apply everywhere and should not be broken. To teach an autistic child to not run across the street, he has to be taught the rule in many different places; the rule has to be generalized and part of that process is making sure the child understands that the rule should not be broken. However, there are times when an absolute adherence to the rule can cause harm. Children also need to be taught that some rules can change depending on the situation. Emergencies are one such category where rules may be allowed to be broken.

Parents, teachers, and therapists can continually teach and reinforce flexible thinking patterns in children with autism. I hope I have provided some ideas on how to do this while still accommodating the visual manner in which they think.

TEACHING CONCEPTS TO CHILDREN WITH AUTISM

Generally, people with autism possess good skills in learning rules, but they can have less developed abstract thinking skills. Dr. Nancy Minshew and her colleagues at the University of Pittsburgh have done research that may help teachers understand how the autistic mind thinks. For the autistic, learning rules is easy, but learning flexibility in thinking is difficult, and must be taught.

There are three basic levels of conceptual thinking: 1) learning rules, 2) identifying categories, and 3) inventing new categories. Category forming ability can be tested by placing a series of objects on a table, such as pencils, notepads, cups, nail files, paper clips, napkins, bottles, videotapes, and other common objects. A person with autism can easily identify all the pencils, or all the bottles. He can also easily identify objects in simple categories, such as all the objects that are green or all the metal objects. Conceptual thinking at this basic level is generally not a problem.

Where the person with autism has extreme difficulty is inventing new categories, which is the beginning of true concept formation. For example, many of the objects in the list referenced above could be classified by use (i.e., office supplies) or by shape (round/not round). To me, it is obvious that a cup, a bottle, and a pencil are all round. Most people would classify a video cassette as not-round; however, I might put it into the round category because of its round spools inside.

One of the easiest ways to teach concept formation is through playing category-forming games with children. For example, a cup can be used to drink from, or to store pencils or paper clips. In one situation, it is used for drinking; in the other, it is used in the office or at work. A videotape can be used for recreation or education, depending on the content of the tape. Notepads can be used for note taking, for art drawings, or, more abstractly, as a paperweight or a coaster for a glass. Activities such as these must be done with a high degree of repetition; it will take some time for the person with autism to learn to think differently. However, with perseverance, results will occur.

Helping children "get into their head" different and varied ways of categorizing objects is the first step in developing flexible thinking. The more examples provided, the more flexible his or her thinking can become. The more flexible the thinking, the easier it will be for the person with autism to learn to develop new categories and concepts. Once the child has acquired some flexible thinking skills with concrete objects, teachers can begin to expand their conceptual thinking into the less concrete areas of categorizing feelings, emotions, facial expressions, etc.

Flexible thinking is a highly important ability that is often—to the detriment of the child—omitted as a teachable skill on a child's IEP. It impacts a child in all environments, both now and in the future: school, home, relationships, employment, recreation. Parents and teachers need to give it more attention when developing a child's educational plan.

Reference

Minshew, N.J., J. Meyer, and G. Goldstein. 2002. Abstract reasoning in autism: a dissociation between concept formation and concept identification. *Neurospychology* 16: 327-334.

BOTTOM-UP THINKING AND LEARNING RULES

Individuals on the autism spectrum learn to form concepts by grouping many specific examples of a particular concept into a virtual "file folder" in their brain. There may be a file folder labeled "Dogs," full of many mental pictures of different kinds of dogs—together, all those mental pictures form a concept of "Dog." A person on the autism spectrum may have many of these virtual file folders in their brain—one for each different concept (rudeness, turn-taking, street safety, etc.). As a person grows older, they create new file folders and add new pictures to the ones in their old file folders.

People on the autism spectrum think differently from non-autistic, or "typical" people. They are "bottom-up," or "specific-to-general" thinkers. For example, they may need to see many, many different kinds of dogs before the concept of dog is permanently fixed in their mind. Or they may need to be told many times, in many places, that they must stop, look, and listen before crossing the street before the concept of street safety is permanently fixed in their mind. People on the spectrum create the concepts of dog, street safety, and everything else by "building" them from many specific examples.

Non-autistic, or "typical" people think in a completely different way. They are "top-down thinkers," or "general-to-specific" thinkers. They form a concept first, and then add in specific details. For example, they already have a general concept of what a dog looks like, and as they see more and more dogs, they add the details of what all kinds of different dogs (poodles, basset hounds, dachshunds, etc.) look like. Once someone tells them to stop, look, and listen before crossing the street, they know to do this at every street, in every neighborhood.

Bottom-up learning can be used to teach both very concrete and more abstract concepts ranging from basic safety rules to reading comprehension. In this chapter I will give examples starting from the most concrete concepts and finishing with more abstract ones. All concepts, regardless of the level of abstraction, must be taught with many specific examples for each concept.

To teach a basic safety rule, such as not running across the street, it must be taught in more than one place. This is required to make the safety rule "generalize" to new places. It must be taught at the street at home, at streets near the school, at the next-door neighbor's house, at streets around grandparents' houses, or Aunt Georgia's house, and when the child visits a new, strange place. The number of different specific examples required will vary from child to child. When I was little, I was taught turn-taking with a board game called Parcheesi. If my turn-taking lessons had been limited to this game they would not have generalized to other situations, such as taking turns with my sister to use a sled or a toy. During all of these activities, I was told I had to take turns. Turn-taking in conversation was also taught at the dining room table. If I talked too long, Mother told me I had to give someone else a turn to talk.

Using many specific examples should also be used for teaching number concepts. To achieve generalization, a child should be taught counting, adding, and subtracting, with many different kinds of objects. You can use cups, candies, toy dinosaurs, pens, Matchbox cars, and other things to teach the abstract idea that arithmetic applies to many things in the real world. For example $5 - 2 = 3$ can be taught with five candies. If I eat 2 of them, I have 3 left. To learn concepts such as less and more, or fractions, try using cups of water filled to different levels, cutting up an apple, and cutting up cardboard circles. If you only used cardboard circles, the child might think that the concept of fractions applies only to cardboard circles. To teach bigger versus smaller, use different-sized objects such as bottles, candies, shirts, blocks, toy cars, and other things.

More Abstract Concepts

To move up a degree in the abstractness of concepts, I will give some examples for teaching concepts such as "up" and "down." Again, you must use many specific examples to teach these concepts.

> The squirrel is "up" in the tree.
> The stars are "up" in the sky.
> We throw the ball "up" in the air.
> We slide "down" the slide.
> We dig a hole "down" in the ground.
> We bend "down" to tie our shoes.

To fully comprehend the concept, the child needs to participate in the activity while the parent or teacher says a short sentence containing the word "up" or "down." Be sure to vocally emphasize the concept word. If the child has difficulty with verbal language, combine the word with a picture card that says "up" or "down."

Recently I was asked, "How did you comprehend the concept of rude behavior or good table manners?" Concepts that relate to judgments or social expectations are much more abstract for a child, yet they can still be taught in the same way. When I did something that was bad table manners, such as waving my fork in the air, Mother explained to me—very simply and without a lot of verbal chatter—that it was bad table manners. "Temple, waving your fork in the air is bad table manners." She used many naturally occurring teachable moments, helping me connect my action to the concept "bad table manners." She did this matter-of-factly and kept the message simple and consistent. Learning many specific examples also worked when she taught me the concept of rudeness. When I did something that was rude, such as belching or cutting in line, Mother told me I was being rude. Gradually a "rude" concept formed in my brain from the many specific examples.

READING COMPREHENSION

Many children on the spectrum can decode and read, but they have problems with comprehension. To start, focus on the very concrete facts, such as characters' names, cities they visited, or activities they did, such as playing golf. This is generally easier for the child to comprehend. Then move on to more abstract concepts in a passage of literature. For example, if they read, "Jim ate eggs and bacon" they may have difficulty answering the multiple-choice question: "Did Jim eat breakfast, lunch, or dinner?" Teach the child to break apart the question and scan his or her brain files for information that may help with comprehension. For instance, I would search through the files in my brain for pictures of meals. A picture of eggs with bacon is the best match for breakfast compared to lunch and dinner pictures.

These more abstract concepts and associations don't develop quickly. The child will need to add more and more information into his brain computer before he can be successful with abstractions. This data comes from experiences, which is why parents and teachers need to give the child lots and lots of opportunities for repetitive practice on a concept or lesson. I would start to learn this sort of concept only after a teacher had explained many different stories to me.

Laying the Foundation for Reading Comprehension

Parents and teachers of children on the autism spectrum tell me all the time that their child or student can read really well but lacks comprehension. This section outlines some of my ideas for laying the foundation for good reading comprehension.

Start with the Concrete

To teach reading comprehension, start with concrete (fact-based) questions about the information in a short story or article. Concrete questions are literal and have a correct answer. Some examples of a concrete question based on a short story about Jane's winter day are "What color is Jane's coat?" or "What town does Jane live in?" Words that would answer these, such as "red" or "Milltown," can be answered from details in the text.

Mix in Abstract Questions

After the student is successful at answering a variety of concrete comprehension questions, progress to asking slightly more abstract questions about a short story. These questions require comprehension of more general concepts. For example, "Jane and Jim went to the store. Jane bought a necklace, and Jim bought a shirt." The question could be, "Did Jim buy clothing?"

An even more abstract level of comprehension is illustrated in a question about the following sentences. "Jim is going on an expedition to Antarctica. The weather is extremely cold there." The question could be, "Will Jim need winter clothes?"

Provide a Variety of Examples

Many children and adults with autism are not able to take all the facts they know and link them together to form concepts. However, they do excel at recognizing individual facts and details. Parents and teachers can use this strength to build reading comprehension.

Bottom-up thinkers learn to generalize and develop concepts by first recognizing details or specific examples, collecting these in their heads, and then putting them into a category to form a concept. This mental process is similar to putting scraps of related information into a common file. Children need to be exposed to many different examples of a general or abstract concept, both in reading and in real-life experiences. For example, my concept of danger (from cars in the street) was formed from seeing a squirrel that had been run over by a car, and this example was followed by many other examples of danger connected to fast-moving vehicles.

Deconstruct Complexity

The same principle applies for more complex reading texts. Comprehension can be taught gradually by pointing out many specific examples that illustrate the larger concept. In college, I called this process "finding the basic principle." I never forgot the concepts my English literature professor taught on deriving meaning from complicated classics. I found his description of Shakespeare, Homer, and other authors super interesting.

In longer reading materials, such as a chapter in a book, the child will need to be able to identify and answer questions about the main idea. The teacher could have the child read passages from a book and then dissect the chapter in a methodical manner for the child so that he understands how the main idea is derived. After the teacher explains the concept the author is conveying, the student will start to understand the concept of finding the main idea of other reading materials. Repeat this process with several other texts to provide the student with ample examples of identifying the main idea.

To help a student understand an author's opinion, a teacher could start with editorials in a newspaper or online publication and then point by point explain how the gist of the author's opinion is determined. For example, an editorial in a local newspaper may be informing citizens of a potential dog park. The author describes the pros and cons of having a dog park, and the student could be guided to categorize each of the author's points under pro and con headings. The comprehension question could be, "Is the author in favor or not in favor of starting a dog park?"

It would be best to start by choosing reading materials where the author's opinion is easy to determine, and then gradually move toward texts where the author's opinion is more nuanced. After several examples, the student should start understanding how to identify an author's opinion.

Another level of complexity is understanding the emotional content of text. The best way to teach this is to take a variety of reading materials and step by step explain how to determine emotional content. An example of emotional content would be, "Jim was smiling and laughing at silly stunts on a reality show." The question could be, "Was Jim happy or sad?"

Regardless of the level of abstraction, reading for comprehension should be taught with many specific examples. How many examples needed will differ for each individual. Teachers and parents can help by giving many opportunities for repetitive practice. Incorporating the bottom-up approach in teaching will give the student time to build a mental file of examples to use when analyzing future reading materials.

MOTIVATING STUDENTS

O ne frequent characteristic of individuals on the autism spectrum is an obsessive interest in one or a few particular subjects, to the exclusion of others. These individuals may be near-genius on a topic of interest, even at a very early age. Parents have described to me their ten-year-old child whose knowledge of electricity rivals that of a college senior, or a near-teen whose knowledge of insects far surpasses that of his biology teacher. However, as motivated as they are to study what they enjoy, these students are often equally unmotivated when it comes to schoolwork outside their area of interest.

It was like this with me when I was in high school. I was totally unmotivated about schoolwork in general. But I was highly motivated to work on the things that interested me, such as showing horses, painting signs, and doing carpentry projects. Luckily, my mother and some of my teachers used my special interests to keep me motivated. Mr. Carlock, my science teacher, took my obsessive interests in cattle chutes and the squeeze machine to motivate me to study science.

The squeeze machine relaxed me. Mr. Carlock told me that if I really wanted to know why the machine had this effect, I would have to study the boring school subjects so that I could graduate and then go to college to become a scientist who could answer this question. Once I really grasped the idea that to get from here to there—from middle school to graduation to college and then to a job of interest to me—I needed to apply myself to all my school subjects, boring or not. This understanding maintained my motivation to complete the work.

While students are in elementary school, teachers can easily keep them involved by using a special interest to motivate their learning. An example would be taking a student's interest in trains and using a train theme in many different subjects. In history class, read about the history of the railroad; in math class, involve trains in problem solving; in science class, discuss different forms of energy that trains utilized then and now, etc.

As students move into middle and high school, they can get turned on by visiting interesting workplaces, such as construction sites, architecture firms, or research labs. This makes the idea of a career real to the student and they begin to understand the education path they must take early on in school to achieve that career. If visiting work sites is not possible, invite parents who have interesting jobs into the school classroom to talk with students about their jobs. Lots of pictures to show what the work is like are strongly recommended. This is also an opportunity for students to hear about the social side of employment, which can provide motivation for making new friends, joining groups or venturing out into social situations that might be uncomfortable at first.

Students on the spectrum need to be exposed to new things in order to become interested in them. They need to see concrete examples of really cool things to keep them motivated to learn.

I became fascinated by optical illusions after seeing a single movie in science class that demonstrated optical illusions. My science teacher challenged me to recreate two famous optical illusions, called the Ames Distorted Room and the Ames Trapezoidal Window. I spent six months making them out of cardboard and plywood and I finally figured them out. This motivated me to study experimental psychology in college.

Bring Trade Magazines to the Library

Scientific journals, trade magazines, and business newspapers can show students a wide range of careers and help turn students on to the opportunities available after they graduate. Every profession, from the most complex to the practical, has its trade journal. Trade magazines are published in fields as diverse as banking, baking, car wash operation, construction, building maintenance, electronics, and many others. Parents who already work in these fields could bring their old trade journals to the school library. These magazines would provide a window into the world of jobs and help motivate students.

Additional Math, Science, and Graphics Resources

About.com's Animation Channel: Free animation software, plus free articles and tutorials. animation.about.com

Foldit: An online game where students can solve protein-folding chemistry problems and make real contributions to medical science.

Khan Academy: Free math and computer programming lessons. Learn JavaScript and other languages.

Code Academy: Free programming lessons

Udacity: Programming classes

Coursera: Online college courses

www.sketchup.com

Udemy.com – free animation courses

Citizen Science Project – National Geographic Society

Citizen Science – NASA

The National Science Digital Library: A national network of learning environments and resources for science, technology, engineering, and mathematics education at all levels. nsdl.org

OpenCourseWare Consortium: Free college course materials. ocwconsortium.org

Physics Education Technology (PhET): Fun, interactive, science simulations, from the PhET project at the University of Colorado. phet.colorado. edu

Wolfram Alpha: A knowledge engine that doesn't find information, but instead computes information based on built-in data, algorithms, and methods. wolframalpha.com

Wolfram MathWorld: A really awesome mathematics site that serves as a wiki encyclopedia of equations, theorems, algorithms, and more. mathworld. wolfram.com

GETTING KIDS TURNED ON TO READING

O ne complaint I am hearing from both parents and teachers is that common core standards makes it impossible to spend much time on subjects other than reading and math because school districts put so much emphasis on students passing tests in these subjects. Recently, I had a discussion with a mom about teaching reading. She told me that her daughter, who has reading problems, was not allowed to go outside for recess because she had to do reading drills. The girl was bored stiff and hated it. However, she quickly learned to read when her mom taught her from a Harry Potter book. To motivate kids, especially those with autism spectrum disorders, you need to start with books the kids want to read. The Harry Potter series is one of the best things that has happened to reading instruction. Two hours before the last Harry Potter book went on sale, I visited the local Barnes and Noble. It was jammed full of kids in costume and a line stretched halfway around the block. I think it is wonderful that the kids were getting so turned on about a book.

I could not read when I was in third grade. Mother taught me to read after school from an interesting book about Clara Barton, a famous nurse. The content kept me interested, and motivated me to learn, even though the book was written at the sixth grade level. Mother taught me how to sound out the words, and within three months, my reading skills jumped two grade levels on standardized tests. One of the things that helped me to learn the phonetic speech sounds was singing the ABC song. That song contains many speech sounds. I was a phonics learner, but other kids on the autism spectrum are visual, sight-word learners. When they read the word dog, they see a picture of a dog in their head. Children are different; parents should identify which way their child learns best and then use that method. There is now scientific evidence that there are separate neural pathways for either visually mapping whole words or decoding them phonologically.

Sight-word readers usually learn nouns first. To learn the meaning of words like went and going I had to see them in a sentence I could visualize. For example, "I went to the supermarket" or "I am going to the supermarket." One is past and the other is future. When I went to the supermarket I see myself with the bag of groceries I purchased. When I say I am going to the supermarket, I see myself driving there. Use examples the child can visualize and relate to when teaching all the connector words that are not easily visualized themselves.

If my third grade teacher had continued trying to teach me to read with endless, boring drills, I would have failed the reading competency tests required by school systems that are "teaching to the test" to obtain better school-wide ranking on standardized tests. After Mother taught me reading, I was able to do really well on the elementary school reading tests. She got me engaged in reading in a way that was meaningful to me until reading became naturally reinforcing on its own.

Parents and teachers can use a child's special interests or natural talents in creative ways to teach basic academic skills such as reading and math. Science and history make wonderfully interesting topics to teach both subjects to spectrum children. If the child likes dinosaurs, teach reading using books about dinosaurs. A simple math problem might be rewritten using dinosaurs as the subject or new exercises created by the adult. For example: if a dinosaur walks at five miles per hour, how far can he walk in fifteen minutes?

Students with ASD can get excellent scores on standardized tests when more creative methods are used that appeal to their interests and ways of thinking. Although this creative effort may take a little more time at the onset, the improved learning, interest and motivation in the child will more than make up for the extra time in the long run.

Reference

Moseley, R.L. et al. (2014). Brain routes for reading in adults with and without autism: EMEG evidence. *J Autism Dev Disord.* 44:137-153.

TOO MUCH VIDEO GAMING AND SCREEN TIME HAS A BAD EFFECT ON CHILD DEVELOPMENT

At conferences, more and more parents of a recently diagnosed teen or elementary school child have told me that they may be on the autism spectrum. In some cases, they have an official diagnoses and in other cases, they do not. Almost all the parents who have been told me that they are on the autism spectrum have worked successfully in a variety of occupations. The question is: why was their life relatively successful, and their child is having problems with lack of friends, bullying, or is extremely hyper and anxious? In most of these cases, the child has no early childhood speech delay. A possible contributor to a poorer prognosis may be excessive use of video games or other on-screen entertainment. When I was in college, I had friends who today would be labeled as having autism. Individuals on the autism spectrum are more likely to have pathological video game use. The ICD-11 now has a formal diagnosis for gaming disorder. Research shows that eight percent of all young people who play video games may be true addicts.

There may be two reasons why both these mildly autistic parents and my geeky classmates got and kept decent jobs.

1. They learned how to work at a young age. I have written extensively about this.
2. In my generation, kids played outside with their peers and learned social interactions. They were not glued to electronic screens.

In the September/October 2016 *Carlat Report of Child Psychiatry*, I read two articles that were a great "light bulb" moment. One was written by Mary G. Burke, M.D., psychiatrist at the Sutter Pacific Medical foundation in San Francisco, and the other was an interview with Michael Robb, PhD of Common Sense Media. Dr. Burke explained that both babies and children need to engage with other people who react to their behavior. The problem with watching endless videos is that the video does not react to the child's responses. Today, Michael Robb recommends no more than 10 hours of screen time a week until the kids are in high school. This is the same rule my mother enforced for TV watching. The American Academy of Pediatrics recommends limited screen time to one to two hours a day. For young children under 18 months, the American Psychological Association recommends no screen time except for video chatting with people they know.

Electronic-Device-Free Times

Both specialists recommend that every family should have specific electronic-device-free times so they can interact and talk. There should be at least one device-free meal per day where both parents and children turn off and put all electronic devices away. In her practice, Dr. Burke has observed that reducing use of electronics reduces symptoms of OCD, panic attacks, and hyperactivity. According to The Centers of Disease Control, the diagnosis of ADHD has increased. Overuse of screens may be a contributor to this problem.

One study showed that a session of five days at an outdoor nature camp with no electronics improved the ability of middle school children to read non-verbal social cues. A farmer who ran a summer camp for eight- to eleven year olds had an interesting observation. During afternoon periods of free play in a walnut orchard, the boys sulked around for the first two days. On the third day, she told me, a switch flipped and they discovered free play. My three recommendations are:

1. Have one electronic-device-free meal each day in which everybody—including parents—puts away all screens.
2. Limit video watching and video games, and other non-school screen time to 10 hours a week.
3. Engage the entire family in activities where people have to interact with each other.

Technology Industry Parents Restrict Electronics

The people who make electronic media in Silicon Valley are greatly restricting their children's use of video games and video watching. Two articles in the *New York Times* and *Business Insider* clearly show that the people who create the technology are concerned about their own children's use of electronics. Research is now showing that people on the autism spectrum are at a greater risk of developing video game addictions. When I talk to parents at autism meetings, I am observing two pathways for fully verbal young adults. The ones with the best outcomes learn how to hold a job before graduation from either high school or college. The ones with the poorest outcomes may play video games for three to eight hours every day. Some of these kids have not been taught basic skills, such as shopping by themselves.

Friends Through Online Multi-Player Games

There are a number of papers that show that games where teens can talk to their friends can have some positive effects. Low to moderate use of multi-player games would be one hour a day on weekdays and two hours a day on weekends. These games, when used in moderation, may help a child make and keep friends. When used properly with parental supervision, the online friendships can be turned into friendships in person. Children need to be taught to plan their play so that they do not have to stop in the middle of a Fortnite match. To do this, they may have to have no video games on one night in order to have sufficient time to complete a match on the next night. Some enterprising parents have developed activities to connect video games back to the real world. They went to the lumberyard and bought wood that was sanded and painted to create MineCraft blocks. One child with autism became the center of attention in his neighborhood with MineCraft blocks in his home's driveway.

There will be some situations where getting a child to disengage from a video game becomes so difficult that the games may have to be banned. A free paper is available online titled "Measuring DSM-5 Internet Gaming Disorder: Development Validation of a Short Psychometric Scale." It has nine questions to help determine if an individual has problem video game use. Some of the internet gaming disorder questions are:

1. Feeling more irritability, anxiety, or sadness when an attempt is made to reduce video game use.
2. Loss of interest in other hobbies or activities.
3. Jeopardizing jobs, education, or career.

How Can Video Games Be Harmful?

Video games can reduce empathy. Realistic killing of people or animals and showing cruelty and gore would be much more damaging than a game where inanimate objects or cartoon characters are destroyed. It is my opinion that images that enable a game player to graphically inflict pain and suffering on realistic human images are likely to be the most damaging. Douglas Gentle at Iowa State University reported that a meta-analysis of 136 scientific articles on violent video games showed that playing them led to desensitization and aggressive behavior (Bavelier et al., 2011). However, I believe that the nature of the violence is important. When I was a child, my hero was the Lone Ranger. He shot lots of bad guys who fell off their horses. In these shows, many people were shot, but they never showed realistic depictions of cruelty or suffering.

Pictures of car crashes or exploding aliens do not bother me. Violence done to objects, such as cars and buildings, does not have the same effect on me as graphic depictions of cruelty and torture. Since I am a visual thinker, I avoid movies that show graphic images of violence or cruelty. I do not want these pictures in my memory. In many movies, I analyze chase scenes and think, "This is impossible. A car cannot crash into a storefront and still be drivable." I am especially concerned when young children play realistic killings games. Little kids need to learn to control aggressive impulses. Canadian researchers have found that some children, especially in disadvantaged homes, show violent tendencies before age six that may lead to criminal behavior unless the child is taught how to control aggression. Dr. Michael Rush at Boston's Children's Hospital can help you determine if your child spends too much time online (See Reddy, 2019).

In conclusion, video game use should be limited. I usually do not recommend banning it. A child needs to have enough experiences so he/she learns that there are many things in the world that are more interesting than video games. Some video game addicts have been successfully weaned off of video games with car mechanics. The individuals discovered that fixing cars was more interesting than video games. This has led to a good career in car mechanics for some video game addicts.

References

Bavelier, D.C., Green, C.S., Han, D.H., Renshaw, P.F., Merzenich, M.M. and Gentile, D.A. (2011). Brains on video games, *Nature Review of Neuroscience* 12(12):763-768.

Bowles, N. (2018) A dark consensus about screens and kids begins to emerge in Silicon Valley, *New York Times*, October 26, 2018.

CDC (2016) Attention-Deficit/Hyperactivity Disorder (ADHD) Data and statistics cdc.gov (accessed June 28, 2019).

Courtwright, D.T. (2019) *The Age of Addiction: How Bad Habits Became Big Business*, Harvard University Press.

Englehardt, C. and Mazurek, M.O. (2013) Video game access, parental rules and problem behavior: A study of boys with autism spectrum disorder, *Autism* (October). 18:529-587.

Englehardt, C. et al. (2017) Pathological game use in adults with and without autism spectrum disorder, *Peer Journal* 5:e3393.

Increasing prevalence of parent reported attention deficit/hyperactivity disorders among children, United States, 2003-2007.

Franklin, N., and Hunt, J. (2012) Rated E – Keeping up with our patient's video game playing, *The Brown University Child and Adolescent Behavior Letter* 28(3):1-5 doi: 10.1002/chi.20159.

Hall, S.S. (2014) The accidental epigenticist, *Science* 505:14-17.

Jargon, J. (2019) Gaming as a social bridge, *The Wall Street Journal*, June 26, 2019, pp. A13.

Kuss, D.J. et al. (2018) Neurobiological correlates in internet gaming disorder: A systematic literature review, *Frontiers in Psychiatry*, 9:166 10:3389/fpsyt.2018.00166.

Mazurek, M., Shattuck, P., Wagner, M., Cooper, B. December 8, 2011, Prevalence and correlates of screen-based media use among youths with autism spectrum disorders. Journal of Autism and Development Disorders. Available at: www.springerlink.comcontent/98412t131480547.

Mazurek, M.O., and Englehardt, C.R. (2013) Video games use in boys with autism spectrum disorder, ADHD or typical development, *Pediatrics* 132:260-266.

Mazurek, M.O. et al. (2015) Video games from the perspective of adults on the autism spectrum disorder, *Computers in Human Behavior*, 51:122-130.

Murray, A. et al. (2021) Gaming disorder in adults with autism disorder. *Journal of Autism and Developmental Disorders*, 52: 2762-2769.

Pontes, H.M. et al. (2015) Measuring DSM-5 internet gaming disorder: Development and validation of a short psychrometric scale. *Computers and Human Behavior*, 45:137-143 http://dx.doi,org/10.1016/j.chb.2014.12.006

Reddy, S. (2019) How to tell if your kids spend too much time online, *The Wall Street Journal*, p. A13, June 18, 2019.

Stone, B.G. et al. (2018) Online multiplayer games for social interactions of children with autism spectrum disorder: A resource for inclusive education, *International Journal of Inclusive Education*, pp. 1-20.

Sundburg, M. (2017) Online gaming loneliness and friendships among adolescents and adults with ASD, *Computers in Human Behavior*, https:doiorg/10.1016/j.chb.2017.10-020

Uhls, Y.T. et al. (2014) Five days at outdoor education camp without screens improves preteen skills with nonverbal emotion cues, *Computers and Human Behavior*, 39:387-392.

Welles, C. (2018) Silicon Valley parents are raising their kids tech free and it should be a red flag, BusinessInsider.com.

THERAPY ANIMALS AND AUTISM

A s I travel around the country to talk with parents of individuals with ASD, more of them are asking whether they should get a service dog for their child with autism. The use of service or assistance dogs with spectrum children is gaining popularity, and there is increasing scientific evidence that service dogs are beneficial. However, this is a complicated issue. Unlike other autism interventions that can be more easily started and stopped, embarking on the journey to find an appropriate service dog for a child is a long-term commitment on the part of the entire family. A service dog is much more than a well-trained pet.

The first question I ask is, "Does your child like dogs?" If the family does not already own a dog, I suggest they see how their child will react to a friend's friendly dog first. There are three kinds of reactions the child can have. The first is an almost magical connection with dogs. The child and the dog are best buddies. They love being together. The second type of reaction is a child who may be initially hesitant but gets to really like dogs. The child should be carefully introduced to a calm, friendly dog. The third type of reaction is avoidance or fear. Often, the child who avoids dogs has a sensory issue. For instance, a child with sensitive hearing may be afraid of the dog's bark because it hurts his/her ears.

When I was a small child, the sound of the school bell hurt my ears like a dentist drill hitting a nerve. To a child with severe sound sensitivity, a dog may be perceived as a dangerous, unpredictable thing that can make a hurtful sound at any moment. For some individuals, the smell of a dog may be overpowering, although keeping the dog clean may alleviate this issue.

I also ask parents if they are willing and able to make the time, financial, and commotional commitment of having a service dog. This is a family affair, with everyone in the family involved. Waiting lists can be two years or more and fees for the trained dog can run $10,000 or more initially, and several thousand dollars each year thereafter.

Types of Service Dogs

There are three basic types of service dogs that are most likely to be used for individuals with autism. They are therapy dogs, a companion dog or a safety dog. A therapy dog is owned by a teacher or therapist and is used during lessons to facilitate learning. A companion dog lives with the family and spends most of its day interacting with the individual with autism. The dog can assist with social, emotional, behavioral, and sensory challenges in the child. These dogs also serve as a "social ice breaker" because other people are often attracted to a dog and will interact more readily with the child. Some individuals with autism really open up and interact with a dog.

Therapy dogs and companion service dogs must have basic obedience training plus training for public access. Companion service dogs usually receive additional training that focuses specifically on the needs of the child for whom it has been matched. For more information on training standards, visit the International Association of Assistance Dog Partners' website (iaadp. org).

The third type of service dog is the safety dog. These are highly trained service dogs used with individuals with severe autism who tend to run off. The child is tethered to the dog and the dog becomes a protector of sorts for the child. Safety dogs have to be used carefully to avoid stressing the dog. These animals need time off to play and just be a dog.

CHAPTER 2: TEACHING & EDUCATION

Dogs that are chosen to be assistance/service dogs should be calm, friendly, and show absolutely no signs of aggression toward strange people. They have to be trained for good manners in public such as not jumping on or sniffing people and not barking. This level of basic training is the absolute minimum any therapy or companion service dogs should obtain. Advanced training to become familiar with the behaviors of people with ASD is preferable.

Rules for Access to Public Places with Dogs

The Americans with Disabilities Act (ADA) has specific rules. A true service dog is allowed in ALL public places. An emotional support dog is not a service dog according to the ADA, but it does have more privileges than a regular dog. To be designated as a service dog, the animal is "trained to do work or perform a task for a person with a disability." It performs a task the person cannot do themselves. A service dog can also do tasks, such as detecting the start of a panic attack. To be designated as an emotional support animal, the person must have a diagnosis from a doctor or mental health professional. People must act responsibly when it comes to their dogs traveling with them. In one horrible case on Delta airlines, an ESA dog ripped up the face of another passenger. Please do not bring dogs that may bite into public areas unless they are muzzled.

Due to several severe biting incidents, emotional support dogs (ESA) are not allowed to travel for free on most airlines. They can travel as a pet, and a fee will have to be paid. Small dogs that can be put in a carrier can travel in the cabin. The carrier must be able to fit under a seat. The airlines require service dog owners to fill out a form from the U.S. Department of Transportation forty-eight hours before their flight. To access it, type the entire title into a search engine: U.S. Department of Transportation Service Animal Transportation Form.

There are many different groups who train companion and service dogs. One of the best ways to find a respectable source is through referrals from satisfied people who have service dogs. It is also important to train the dog to know the difference between work and play behavior. A dog's brain will create categories of behavior. When the vest is on, he works, and when the vest is off, it's time to play. The dog needs to be taught clear "vest on" and "vest off" behavior.

Questions to Ask when Selecting a Service Dog Provider

- What breeds of dogs do you use for autism assistance dogs?
- Can we (the family) assist in selecting the dog for our child?
- Do you start the process with puppies, or are your placements fully grown dogs?
- If puppies, what will happen if my child doesn't take to the dog? What if the dog's maturing personality becomes mismatched to my child?
- If an adult dog (two years or older), has the dog been trained specifically with ASD behaviors in mind, or has training been generalized to people with other disabilities instead?
- Describe the training program the dog receives. How long does it last and to what extent is our family involved?
- Does the training address socialization issues only, or are the dogs trained to handle run away situations, sensory sensitivities, behavioral challenges, emergency situations, etc.?
- Will the dog be trained with my child's specific needs/behaviors in mind?

- At what age will the dog come into our home?
- Has/will the dog be trained to respond to hand signals in addition to verbal commands? This is especially important if the child is nonverbal or has limited verbal skills.
- How many dog placements with children with autism has your organization completed?
- How successful were these placements over time?
- How much family training with the dog is required/provided to us? Does this include training with the spectrum child, or just with parents?
- Is there any "refresher" training provided at a future date?
- What type of ongoing communication with our family will be included once the dog is placed?
- Do you have references of families of children with ASD who own one of your dogs?
- What is your application procedure?
- Is there a waiting list, and if so, for how long?
- What are your fees for an assistance dog? Is there any financial assistance available for this? Do you provide a payment plan over time?
- What type of expenses will our family incur over time in keeping the dog?

Therapy Dogs and Horses

There is increasing evidence that dogs, horses, and other animals can have definite therapeutic benefits. Animals that are used in therapy are often not trained service animals. For individuals with autism, dogs and horses can be really helpful in teaching social skills. A paper by Carolien Wijker (2019) takes an extensive look at this subject. Scientific research shows that equine therapy definitely has benefits. A review of the scientific literature showed that it improved behavior skills and social communication. Another study showed that equine activities and riding improved social motivation and reduced irritability. A third study showed that it had a calming effect.

Therapeutic riding is also becoming increasingly popular. When I was a teenager, my social life revolved around horses and I learned work skills by cleaning stalls. Many studies, including randomized trials show social benefits for individuals with autism. Real horse activities were much more effective than using a fake horse and barn activities with no horses present. I have observed many therapeutic riding programs. Sometimes there is a tendency to over accommodate a rider. I have observed many riders who still have a side walker who were capable of independent riding. Many parents overprotect their children, and activities such as therapeutic riding often prove to them that their child is capable of doing many things.

References and Additional Reading

Becker, J. and Rogers, E.C. (2017) Animal assisted social skills training for children with autism spectrum disorder, *Anthrozoos*, 302:307-326.

Berry, A. et al. (2013) Use of assistance and therapy dogs of children with autism spectrum disorders, *Journal of Alternative and Complimentary Medicine* 18:1-8.

Borgi, M. et al. (2016) Effectiveness of standardized equine assisted therapy program for children with autism spectrum disorder, *Journal of Autism and Developmental Disorder*, 46:1-9.

Brannon, S. et al. (2019) Service animals and emotional support animals where they are allowed and under what condition? ADA National Network, Information Guidance and Training in the American with Disabilities Act.

Burrows, K.E., Adams, C.L. and Millman, S.T. (2008) Factors affecting behavior and welfare of service dogs for children with autism spectrum disorder, *Journal of Applied Animal Welfare Science*, 11:42-62.

Burrows, K.E., Adams, C.L. and Spiers, J. (2008) Sentinels of safety: Service dogs ensure safety and enhance freedom and well-being for families with autistic children, *Quality Health Research*, 18:1642-1649.

Gabnals, R.L. et al. (2015) Randomized controlled trial of therapeutic horseback riding in children and adolescents with autism spectrum disorder, *American Academy of Child and Adolescent Psychiatry*, 54:541-549.

Grandin, T. (2011) The roles animals can play with individuals with autism, In: Peggy McCardle et al. (editors) *Animals in Our Lives*, Brookes Publishing, Baltimore, MD.

Grandin, T (2019) Case Study: How horses helped a teenager with autism make friends and learn how to work, *International Journal of Environmental Research and Public Health*, 16(13) 2325, doi.org/10.3390/ jerph16132325.

Grandin, T., Fine, A.H. and Bowers, C.M. (2010) The use of therapy animals with individuals with autism, Third Edition, Therapeutic Foundations and Guidelines for Practice, A.H. Fine (Editor) *Animal Assisted Therapy*, Academic Press, San Diego, CA, 247-264.

Gross, P.D. (2005) *The Golden Bridge: A Guide to Assistance Dogs for Children Challenged by Autism and Other Developmental Disorders*, Purdue University Press, West Lafayette, IN.

Harris, A. et al. (2017) The impact of horse-riding intervention on the social functioning of children with autism spectrum disorder, *International Journal of Environmental Public Health*, 14:776.

Llambias, C. et al. (2016) Equine assisted occupational therapy: Increasing engagement in children with autism spectrum disorder, *American Journal of Occupational Therapy*, 70, doi:10.5014/ajot.2016.02070.

O'Hare, M.E. (2013) Animal assisted intervention and autism spectrum disorders: A systematic literature review, *Journal of Autism and Developmental Disorders*, 43:1602-1622.

O'Hare, M.E. (2017) Research on animal assisted intervention and autism spectrum disorder, *Applied Developmental Science*, 21:200-215.

Pavlides, M. (2008) *Animal Assisted Interactions*, Jessica Kingsley Publishers, London, England.

Peters B.C. et al. (2022) Preliminary efficiency of occupational therapy in an equine environment for youth with autism spectrum disorders, *Journal of Autism and Developmental Disorders*, 52(9): 4114-4128

Peters, B.C. et al. (2022) Self-regulation mediates therapeutic horseback riding social functioning outcomes in youth with autism spectrum disorder, *Frontiers in Pediatrics.*

Srinivasan, S.M. et al. (2018) Effects of equine therapy on individuals with autism spectrum disorder: A systematic review, *Review Journal of Autism Developmental Disorders,* 5:156-158.

Trzmiel, T. et al. (2019) Equine assisted activities and therapies in children with autism spectrum disorders: a systemic review and meta-analysis, *Complementary Therapies in Medicine,* 42: 104-113.

Viau, R. et al. (2010) Effects of service dogs on salivary cortisol secretion in autistic children, *Psychoneuroendrocrinology,* 35:1187-1193.

Wijkes, C. et al. (2019) Effects of dog assisted therapy for adults with autism spectrum disorders: An exploratory randomized controlled trial, *Developmental Disorders,* doi.org/10.007/s10803-01903971-9.

Further Information

Autism Service Dogs of America (Autismservicedogsofamerica.org)

Therapy Dogs International (www.tdi-dog.org)

4 Paws 4 Ability (4pawsforability.org/autismdogs.html)

Assistance Dogs International

Assistancedogsinternational.org

Canine Companions for Independence

Canine.org

Paws Giving Independence (www.givingindependence.org)

NEADS World Class Service Dogs (Neads.org)

Assistance Dogs for Autism (Autismassistancedog.com)

Pawsitivity Service Dogs (Pawsitivityservicedogs.com)

THE IMPORTANCE OF CHOICES

S ometimes it is difficult to get children and teens on the spectrum to do new things or participate in everyday activities. When I was afraid to go to my aunt's ranch, Mother gave me the choice of going for either two weeks or all summer. Giving me a choice helped prevent the problem of the option to say "no." Individuals on the spectrum often do better when they have some options or control over their environment. Many parents have told me that their child will often say "no" and refuse to do something. Allowing the child to have some choices will help prevent a lot of stubbornness or oppositional behavior. When there is a choice, it is difficult for the child to answer with "no."

The Right School for Me

My mother allowed me to have choices about how I was going to participate in a new situation. After I was kicked out of a large girl's school because I retaliated for teasing by throwing a book at another girl, my mother had to find a new school for me. Fortunately, she had worked as a TV journalist on two documentaries, so she had already visited many specialized schools in a three-state area near where we lived. First, she narrowed down the list of possibilities by choosing three schools she had visited that she really liked. I had the chance to visit all three schools. I had extensive tours so I could find out what the schools were really like. Then, mother allowed me to pick one of the three schools.

Limiting Access to Video Games

For some children, it will be essential to limit their time spent on video games. One good way to do this is by establishing the length of time a video game can be accessed and then allowing the child to decide when he will use the allotted time to do so. A child could be given a choice of playing the game for one hour when he returns home from school. This could be effective in helping him calm down from a long day at school. Or, the child could choose to play the game for one hour after homework is done. No matter which choice the child makes, he is still playing for only one hour.

Personalizing Personal Hygiene

There is a scene in the movie *Temple Grandin* where my boss slams down a deodorant stick and says, "You stink; use it." This actually happened! Hygiene is often a major issue with teenagers on the spectrum. One way this can be approached is to give the teen some choices of hygiene products to use. What is nonnegotiable is that the teen will have to take a bath or shower every day. However, he can go to the store and choose the soaps or products he will use.

In the past, the selection of hygiene products was limited. I hated the gooey sticky roll-on deodorants that were common in the 1970s. Today there is a wide assortment of products to choose from. (I like the solid, unscented deodorant stick the best.) Scent can also be a big issue in the hygiene product department: it's important that the scent is not overpowering to the individual, or the product is less likely to be used!

Acquisition of Daily Living Skills

There are lots of skills that kids have to learn (e.g., getting dressed, table manners, and household chores). Getting the child to comply is often easier if choices are provided in conjunction with the daily living skills.

Getting dressed. Often getting ready in the morning can be a struggle for young kids on the spectrum. It can be as simple as allowing the child a choice between two different shirts. I chose my clothes and laid them out the night before.

Table manners. At the dinner table, mother insisted on good manners. At the end of the meal, I had a choice. I could ask to be excused early with no dessert or wait and get dessert. Those were the two choices. Leaving early and getting dessert was not allowed.

Household chores. When children feel like they have some say in things, they are much more likely to want to learn and practice skills such as cleaning, picking up toys, and loading the dishwasher. If three chores need to be completed before a child has free time, you could let the child choose the order the chores will be completed in.

It is important to give children choices because many individuals have a reflex reaction to say "no." Letting the child have choices will give his mind time to stop and think instead of going into a reflexive "no" mode. Finesse the "no" with choices, and everyday life can flow much more smoothly for parent and child.

Remember a basic principle in working with autistic individuals: an obsession or fixation has huge motivational potential for the child.

THE IMPORTANCE OF PRACTICAL PROBLEM-SOLVING SKILLS

Both normal children and kids on the autism spectrum need to be challenged. Those who have heard me speak or read my books know I think many parents and educators coddle their children with ASD far more than they should. Children with ASD don't belong in a bubble, sheltered from the normal experiences of the world around them. Sensory issues do need to be taken into consideration, but aside from those, parents may need to push their child a little for any real advancement in learning to occur.

This is especially true in teaching a pivotal life skill: problem-solving. It involves training the brain to be organized, break down tasks into step-by-step sequences, relate parts to the whole, stay on task, and experience a sense of personal accomplishment once the problem is solved. Young kids learn by doing, and kids with ASD often learn best with concrete, visible examples. When I was a child growing up in the '50s, I built tree houses and went on backyard campouts with other neighborhood children. In those situations, several children had to work together to figure out how to accomplish the task. We had to find lumber for the tree house, design it, take measurements, and discuss how to get the boards up the tree and nailed into place. We learned by trying different things; some things worked, others did not.

Experiments with wetting lumber to make it easier to cut with a hand saw were a complete failure.

From our experiences, we learned that dry lumber was easier to cut. The rigorous turn-taking training I had when I was 3 to 6 years old served me well in these group activities. In our family we played lots of board games—an excellent teaching method for learning how to take turns. Turn-taking helped me understand that people can work together for a common purpose, that what one person did could affect me and the outcome of the game positively or negatively. It made me aware of different perspectives, which in turn helped me become a better detective when I had to solve a problem.

I can remember the huge planning meetings we had for the backyard campout. There was candy and soda that had to be bought. We all had to figure out how to put up an old army tent. None of the parents helped, which made it a valuable learning experience for us all.

Like myself, many kids with ASD have a natural curiosity about certain things. These interests can be used constructively to practice problem-solving skills. I loved toys that flew. On a windy day, a parachute I made from a scarf would fly for hundreds of feet. But not on the first try. It took many attempts before I was successful. I had to figure out how to prevent the strings from tangling when I threw the parachute up into the air. I tried building a cross from two pieces of 5" coat-hanger wire to tie the four strings to; it worked. When I was in high school, I was fascinated with optical illusions. After seeing an illusion called the Ames Trapezoidal Window, I wanted to build one. My science teacher challenged me to try to figure it out by myself rather than giving me a book with a diagram. I spent six months working on it, without success. Then my teacher let me have a brief glimpse at a photo in a textbook that showed how the illusion worked. He gave me a hint without telling me exactly how to do it. He helped me develop problem-solving skills.

Children with ASD (and many of their parents) struggle with problem-solving skills today. This may be partially due to us, as a society, doing less hands-on practical work and activities than did our counterparts when I was growing up. We fix less; we toss things out that don't work and buy new ones. Even in today's internet world, there is a need for problem-solving skills. The key is to start with concrete, hands-on projects that have meaning for the child, then slowly move into abstract problem-solving involving thoughts and creativity, in academics and social situations. The ability to solve problems helps a person categorize and use the vast amounts of information in his mind, and from outside sources like the internet, in a successful, intelligent manner. These are important life skills and parents should start early in incorporating problem-solving opportunities into their child's daily routine.

The ability to produce work that pleases others is an essential skill for successful employment.

LEARNING TO DO ASSIGNMENTS THAT OTHER PEOPLE APPRECIATE

Recently I was looking through my old high school album. As I looked through my old photos, I realized I had learned an important skill by the time I was in high school that some people on the autism spectrum never learn. I had photo after photo of projects I had created that pleased others. There was a gate I had built for my aunt out at the ranch and sets I had made for the school play. There were also before and after pictures of the ski tow house I refurbished at my boarding school. Originally, we had a homemade rope to tow an ugly, plywood shed. I put tongue and groove wood siding on the ski tow house, stained it, and then installed white trim around the windows and door. It was decorated the way others would like it. Left to my own preferences, I would have painted pictures of goofy cartoons on it, but that would not have earned the approval of my teachers. In all three projects, I created things taking into consideration the thoughts and preferences of others in my environment. The end result was positive recognition for my work.

During my elementary school years, my mother, my nanny, and my teachers taught me—first in direct and later in indirect ways—that sometimes you can do things to please just yourself, but other times you need to do things that others would like. They also made sure I understood that sometimes this was a choice, while at other times it was mandatory. This is an important and pivotal life skill, and it's an advantage if you can learn it early in childhood. It affects whether or not a child is accepted by his or her peer group, and how well he can work with others. Even as a young child I did projects that pleased others. When I was in fourth grade, I sewed costumes for the school play with my little toy sewing machine. I quickly learned in school that, in order to get good grades, I needed to attend to my teachers' requests, and follow directions. It did no good to turn in a brilliant report if I hadn't addressed the assignment.

Both as a young child and throughout my high school years I was motivated by two factors. The first was getting recognition from others and, secondly, I enjoyed seeing my creations being used in places and events that were important to me.

As children grow into young adults, the ability to produce work that pleases others is an essential skill for successful employment. Students on the spectrum should be taught these essential skills well before they graduate from high school. The teaching should start early, while the child is young, in concrete ways. Educators and parents must teach these individuals to successfully complete assignments that fit somebody else's specifications. If a student is in a robotics club, he has to learn to make a robot that will do an assigned task. A student in middle school English class must learn to write an essay that addresses the specific question posed, even when it's not something interesting to him.

Recently I met a bright man with autism who had just graduated from college. He had absolutely no work experience while he was in high school and college, and absolutely no idea of how to get and keep a job. He had never mowed somebody else's lawn or worked in a store. Other than academics, he had never been put into situations where he needed to satisfactorily produce work according to someone else's directions. By the time I graduated from college I had already done many jobs and internships. Mother realized that preparing me for the world outside my home needed to start slowly and easily, and build, one event, one project, one skill upon another.

Teachers, parents, and therapists must help high-functioning students on the spectrum learn how to do projects to another person's specification. I did not realize how well I had learned this skill until I looked at my old high school photos. This hindsight helped me further realize how much I have grown and developed since then.

LEARNING NEVER STOPS

A fter I turned 50, many people told me my talks kept getting better and smoother. One thing many people do not realize about people on the autism spectrum is that they never stop growing and developing. Each day I learn more and more about how to behave and communicate.

Autistic thought is bottom-up thinking instead of top down, as it is in most people. To form a concept, I put lots of little pieces of information together. The normal person forms a concept first and then attempts to make all the details fit. The older I get, the more data I collect, and the better I become at forming concepts. Being exposed to many new experiences has helped me load more information into the database in my mind, my memory. I have more and more information to help me know how to deal with new situations. To understand something new, I have to compare it to something I have already experienced.

Internet in My Head

The best analogy to how my mind works is this: it is like having an internet inside my head. The only way my internal internet can get information is through reading or actual experiences. My mind also has a search engine that works like Google for pictures. When somebody says a word, I see pictures in my imagination. I have to have visual images to think. When I was younger, the library of pictures in my head was much smaller, so I had to use visual symbols to understand new concepts. In high school, I used door symbols to represent thinking about my future. To think about my future after high school, I practiced walking through an actual door that symbolized my future. Without the door symbol, my future was too abstract for me to understand.

Today I no longer use door symbols because they have been replaced with pictures of other things I have experienced or things I have read. When I read a book with descriptive text, I translate it into photorealistic pictures. As more and more different things are experienced, the more flexible my thinking becomes because the "photo internet" in my head has more pictures and information to surf through.

Exposure to New Things is Essential

Exposing children and adults on the autism spectrum to new things is really important. Mother was always making me try new things, and some I did not like, but I still did them. When I was about twelve years old, Mother enrolled me in a children's sailboating program, two afternoons a week, all summer. It was a poorly run program and I hated it after the first few sessions because I had no buddy to do it with, yet I completed all the sessions. The lesson I learned was that if you start something, you have to finish it.

As an adult I motivate myself to keep learning through extensive reading and personal/professional experiences. In the last ten years of my life, from my fifties to my sixties, I have still improved. One revelation I had around age fifty was learning that humans use little eye signals that I did not know existed. I learned about eye signals from the book, *Mindblindness* by Simon Baron-Cohen. When I read autism literature I gain great insight from both personal accounts of people on the autism spectrum and neuroscience research. Scientific research has helped me understand how my brain is different. That has helped me comprehend "normal" people better.

Doing Assignments

A few years ago I realized the extent to which the training I had in my childhood and teens really helped me later in life. High school was torture with the incessant teasing, and I was a goof-off student with little interest in studying. For years I have written about how my science teacher motivated me to study so I could become a scientist. His mentoring was extremely important. Lately I have realized that although I was not studying in school, I had very good work skills that helped me later in the world of employment. I did lots of work that other people appreciated. I cleaned the horse stalls, shingled the barn roof, and painted signs. Even though I got obsessed with these activities, it was useful work that other people wanted done.

To be successful, people on the spectrum have to learn how to take their skills and do an assignment. The ability to do an assignment (follow directions, stay on task, complete it in a satisfactory manner) was taught to me from a young age. In grade school, my ability in art was encouraged but I was repeatedly asked to create pictures of many different things (again, producing work for others). I enjoyed the praise I got when I drew a picture of something somebody else had requested.

Parents and teachers can lay the groundwork for a child's later success in life by exposing the child to many new experiences. But children and adults of all ages can continue to grow and evolve in their behavior and thinking. It is never too late to expand the mind of a person on the autism spectrum.

TEMPLE GRANDIN earned her PhD in animal science from the University of Illinois and is currently a Professor at Colorado State University. Dr. Grandin is one of the most respected individuals with high-functioning autism in the world. She presents at conferences nationwide, helping thousands of parents and professionals understand how to help individuals with autism, Asperger's syndrome, and PDD. She is the author of *Emergence: Labeled Autistic, Thinking in Pictures, Animals in Translation* (which spent many weeks on *The New York Times* Best-Seller List), *The Autistic Brain*, and *The Loving Push*, co-written with Debra Moore, PhD. One of the most celebrated—and effective—animal advocates on the planet, Dr. Grandin revolutionized animal movement systems and spearheaded reform of the quality of life for the world's agricultural animals.